AUSTRALIAN HISTORY COMPREHENSION YEAR 5

Gunter Schymkiw

Five Senses Education Pty Ltd
2/195 Prospect Highway
Seven Hills 2147
New South Wales
Australia

Copyright © Five Senses Education Pty Ltd 2017
First Published 2017

Schymkiw, Gunter
Australian History Comprehension Year 5

ISBN 978-1-76032-121-5

CONTENTS

I. GRANNY SMITH APPLES

Nature is always surprising us. This is a true story of an amazing change made by nature. The change gave us a new, pleasant tasting fruit.

Maria Ann Smith and her husband came to Australia from England in 1839. They settled on a farm at Ryde near Sydney. It was here that they raised chickens and cows and also had an orchard of apple trees.

One day in 1868 Maria noticed an unusual looking tree. It was growing where, a few years earlier, she had thrown the scraps of some old Tasmanian cooking apples.

As she watched the unusual tree growing, she saw that its apples were different to any she had ever seen before. Even when the apples were mature their skins kept their green colouring.

She tasted one and was pleased to find that it did not taste sour like a cooking apple. She decided to take her apples to market to sell. The apples were very popular and sold well at the market. Today we call them Granny Smith Apples after the lady who first grew them.

Comprehension

A. Write short answers to these.

1. Where did Granny Smith live before she came to Australia?_____

2. Where was her farm located? _____

3. Name three things grown on her farm. _____

4. How did she find out if other people liked her apples?_____

B. Highlight the title that is most suitable for this text.

1. A Wonder Of Nature – The Granny Smith Apple

2. How You Grow Granny Smith Apples

3. Great Australian Inventors – The Woman Who Invented Granny Smith Apples

C. List the following using the text.

1. Granny Smith's two given names: _____

2. Two countries mentioned in the text. _____

D. Find words in the text with these meanings.

The first letter is given in each.

1. a place where fruit trees are grown   **O**_____

2. strange   **U**_____

3. wife's partner   **H**_____

4. selling place   **M** _____

5. well – liked   **P**_____

E. Write a brief description of a Granny Smith apple.

Mention at least 3 things (shape colour, taste, texture, what's inside etc.)

_____

_____

_____

_____

_____

_____

_____

_____

_____

_____

_____

INDICATORS AND OUTCOMES

a. answers literal questions

b. understands the main idea of a story

c. identifies characters and places in a text

d. uses context to work out the meaning of words

e. can write a simple description

Write instructions for making an apple pie. Follow the steps shown by the pictures. Some words are given to help you.

1. pick, place, basket

2. wash, knife, peel

3. slice, core

4. flour, eggs, milk

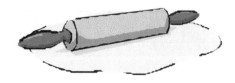

5. rolling pin, pastry, flat

6. baking dish

7. decorate, oven, degrees

8. eat

How to make an Apple Pie

2. LIFESAVERS

Most Australians live on the coast. In the summertime many people visit the beach. Swimming in the surf can be dangerous.

Australia's beaches are among the safest in the world thanks to the unpaid work done by more than ten thousand lifesavers. These people patrol our beaches and often risk their own lives helping swimmers who get into difficulties in the surf.

When, in 1902, Mr William Gocher decided it would be a good idea to go bathing at Manly Beach in New South Wales, he started a trend. The popularity of bathing spread.

In 1907 the New South Wales Surf Bathing Association was formed. Regular beach patrols soon followed. When you next go to the beach say 'hello' to the lifesavers. They may not be able to speak to you because they will be busily watching the water in case someone gets into trouble. They are everyday heroes.

Surfing is believed to have originated in the islands of Polynesia hundreds of years ago. The first record of it being seen by Europeans was by French sailors in Tahiti in 1767 It became very popular with American and Australian youth in the early 1960s and remains popular to this day. A specialized vocabulary has evolved among young surfers.

Comprehension

A. Choose words from the word bank to complete the cloze activity.

sun wet doctor safe untidy

lifesavers hot beach dangerous sharks

Many people in Australia get relief from the _____ weather in summer by

going to the _____. Swimming in the ocean can be _____.

Luckily our beaches are patrolled by _____. They do an important job

and keep our beaches _____.

B. Write short answers to the questions below.

1. Who started the bathing trend in Australia? _____

2. In what year did he do this? _____

3. What was formed in 1907? _____

C. Find words with these meanings in the text. Some letters are given.

1. least dangerous   __ __ **f** __ __ __

2. made up his mind   __ __ **c** __ __ __ __

3. came after   __ __ __ __ __ **w** __ __

4. talk   __ __ __ **a** __

5. difficulty   __ **r** __ __ __ __ __

D. NOUNS are naming words.

List the five nouns in the first two sentences.

_____

_____

VERBS are doing words. List the two verbs that appear in the first two sentences

_____

_____

E. Follow the directions to complete the picture.

1. Draw a sandy beach.

2. Draw three children playing on the beach.

3. Draw some waves.

4. Draw a surfer riding a wave.

5. Draw two clouds.

6. Draw three seagulls in the air.

7. Colour the picture.

Puzzle 1

The words in the word bank are all examples of surfing slang. Match them with their meanings. The highlighted letters (1 to 12) spell out the name of a famous surfer from Newcastle, NSW. Use the internet to check their meanings and complete the puzzle.

> **Kahuna woodie toes grommet huarache catch wipeout**
>
> **surf's up bombora tube curl breaker hang goofy**
>
> **gremlin soup baggies ankle busters walking ding**

1. A __ __ __ __ __ __ __ is a beginning surfer.

2. When we want to say you ride a wave we say you __ __ __ __ __ it.

3. The part of a wave that is curved and breaking is the __ __ __ __.

4. __ __ __ __ __ __ is the Hawaiian god of the surf, sun and sand.

5. A breaking wave is known as a __ __ __ __ __ __ __.

6. If you fall from your surfboard you are said to have a __ __ __ __ __ __ __.

7. __ __ __ __ __ __ __ __ sandals are popular with American surfers. They are made of leather but have soles made from the tread of car tyres. (They are mentioned in the surfing song Surfin' USA by the popular group called The Beach Boys.)

8. To __ __ __ __ five is to place five toes over the front of a surfboard while riding a wave.

9. __ __ __ __ __ __ __ are loose fitting swimming trunks.

10. A __ __ __ __ __ __ __ __ is another name for a beginning surfer. (Different answer to example one.)

11. A __ __ __ __ __ __ __ is a car that was very popular with surfers. It was a station wagon dating from the 1940s and 1950s and parts of its body were made of wood.

12. When the surfing conditions were good surfers would call, ' __ __ __ __ ' __ __ __ !'

PUZZLE 1 ANSWER: __ __ __ __ __ __ __ __ __ __ __ __ __.

Puzzle 2

The highlighted letters (13 to 20) spell out the name of the pop group who had hit songs with the surfing songs, Wipeout and Surfer Joe. Use the internet to check their meanings and complete the puzzle.

13. The white foam caps on some waves are known by surfers as __ __ __ __ .

14. A large hollow curved wave is called a __ __ __ __ by surfers.

15. A wave breaking over a submerged reef is called a __ __ __ __ __ __ __ by Australian surfers.

16. A surfer is known as a __ __ __ __ __ footer if they ride with the right foot forward on the board.

17. __ __ __ __ __ __ __ the board is moving forwards and backwards on the board to keep balance.

18. __ __ __ __ __ __ __ __ __ __ __ are small waves.

19. A __ __ __ __ is the name given to a crack or similar imperfection on the surface of a surfboard.

20. If you ride with __ __ __ __ upon the nose it means your toes are hanging over the front of the board as you ride it.

PUZZLE 2 ANSWER __ __ __ __ __ __ __ __

INDICATORS AND OUTCOMES	a. retells interpretation of a text
	b. answers literal questions
	c. uses context to work out word meanings
	d. identifies grammatical features of a text
	e. follows written directions accurately

3. CRAIG JOHNSTON

Craig Johnston grew up on the shores of Lake MacQuarie, near Newcastle in New South Wales. He was a member of a talented soccer team at Booragul High School (recently re – named Lake MacQuarie High School). Craig said that there was a number of players in the school team that had more natural talent than him. What made Craig an exceptional player was his dedication. When he realised he was not as skilled with his left foot as he was with his right, he spent long hours kicking a ball against a wall using his left foot only. Soon he was as skilful with his left foot as he was with his right.

At 14 years of age Craig took a huge gamble. He went to England, leaving his parents' home, to take up an apprenticeship as a professional footballer with Middlesborough Football Club. This may sound glamorous, but it involved doing many unpleasant jobs like cleaning the mud from the boots of the senior players. Apprentice footballers really did start at the bottom.

An apprentice who did not succeed usually finished up with little money and an interrupted education. Craig often thought that this may be the way he would finish. He was not always encouraged by some members of the coaching staff and felt he could lose his job at Middlesborough at any moment.

The love and support he was given from his family back in Australia helped him keep his courage up. Craig eventually forced his way into Middlesborough's senior team. His good form in the senior football clubs soon attracted interest from other teams. Several offers were made for the young Australian nicknamed Roo.

In 1981, Liverpool, one of the greatest clubs in the world, paid Middlesborough a huge sum to have Craig play for them. In 1986 Craig scored the winning goal for Liverpool in the most important game of the English football season, the FA (short for Football Association) Cup. Liverpool also won the European Cup that year, making them the top club in all of Europe.

Craig surprised many people when he retired from the game in 1988. Even though he was at his peak as a player, he felt it was more important that he return to Australia to help his family look after his sister who had become ill. You can read the story of Craig's life as a footballer in his book, Walk Alone. It is the story of a fine young man and a wonderful family.

Multimedia

You can find out much more about Craig and his career on the Liverpool Football Club site. To find the site search for www.liverpoolfc.com

Can you find the name of Liverpool's home ground? Write it here: _____

Find some footage of some of Craig's goals by clicking on *100 Players Who Shook the Kop.*

What number does Craig have on this list? _____

Liverpool Football Club visited Australia for a friendly game against Melbourne Victory (an Australian club side) in 2013. The crowd sang an emotional version of Liverpool's adopted song, You'll Never Walk Alone. You may be able to view this by typing a search for Melbourne Kop Sing YNWA . See if you are able to view this. Give the song a rating out of 10. _____/ 10

This song was written by Richard Rogers in 1945. Probably the best known version of the song was by an English pop group of the 1960s called Gerry And The Pacemakers. See if you can find this version on a music site. Give it a rating out of 10. _____/ 10

See if you can find the lyrics searching the opening words when you walk through a storm. In a few sentences tell how this song made you feel.

_____

_____

_____

_____

Comprehension

A. Write short answers to these questions:

1. Which high school did Craig attend? _____

2. With which team was Craig an apprentice footballer? _____

3. In which team did Craig play when they won the FA and European Cup finals?

   _____

4. Why did Craig retire in 1988? _____

B. Craig sometimes felt so homesick that he wanted to give up his apprenticeship and go back home to Australia.

Imagine you are in the same position as he was.
Give some reasons he may have given himself for staying or going.

1. I'll go because

   _____

2. I'll stay because

   _____

C. Find words with these meanings in the passage.

The first letter is given.

1. outstanding   **E** _____

2. risk   **G**_____

3. finally   **E** _____

4. finished working   **R**_____

D. These thumbprint characters are playing football (soccer). Fill in the features on those not already done. Do your own thumbprint picture on a piece of paper. You will need an inked stamp pad.

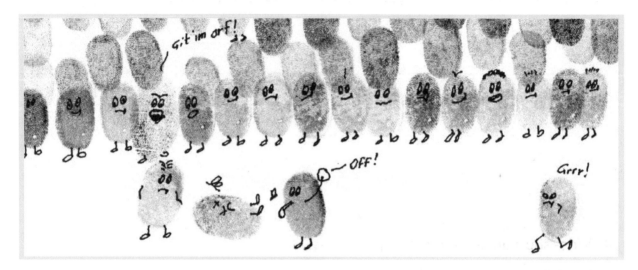

E. Do some research to find the origins of the word **soccer.**

_____

_____

Activity

The words in the word bank all have something to do with soccer (football). Match them with their meanings. The highlighted letters spell out the name of a famous English soccer club. Use an online dictionary to check meanings. When you have done this complete the puzzle.

> **pass   Rimet   shy   striker   stopper   rules   eleven   whistle   sweeper   referee spectators   pea   spherical   Socceroos   gloves   four   penalty   dribbling   yellow corner   red   goalkeepers**

1. The ___ __ __ __ __ __ in a soccer team is the last defender, positioned between the goalkeeper and the rest of the team.

2. The centre – half (number 5) in a soccer team is usually key defender. This position is also sometimes called the __ __ __ __ __ __ __.

3. A __ __ __ __ __ __ __ __ is a free kick awarded because the rules have been infringed.

4. Sometimes goalkeepers wear __ __ __ __ __ __ to assist in gripping the ball.

5. Sometimes a player is warned for seriously infringing the rules by the referee by being shown a __ __ __ __ __ __ card.

6. If you are shown two yellow cards in a match the referee then shows you a __ __ __ card. This means that you must leave the field and no longer participate in the match.

7. A throw in on the sideline is also known as a __ __ __.

8. The __ __ __ __ __ __ __ __ __ __ __ in both teams are the only players who can touch the ball with the hands when it is in play.

9. The World Cup is played for between countries. It was the idea of Jules __ __ __ __ __. The trophy that is played for bears his name.

10. A soccer ball is __ __ __ __ __ __ __ __ in shape.

11. People watching a game are called __ __ __ __ __ __ __ __ __ __.

12. The Australian team is called the __ __ __ __ __ __ __ __ __.

13. There are __ __ __ __ __ __ players in a soccer team.

14. The referee uses a __ __ __ __ __ __ __ to control play in a soccer match.

15. A kick to a team mate is called a __ __ __ __.

16. If you miss kick a ball so that it goes behind your goal line but not between the goalposts your opposing team is given a free kick that is known as a __ __ __ __ __ __.

17. Moving a ball with the feet using short kicks is called __ __ __ __ __ __ __ __ __.

18. The cork ball inside a whistle is called the __ __ __.

19. The Football Association met in 1863 to draw up the __ __ __ __ __ of soccer.

20. The __ __ __ __ __ __ __ is in charge of administering the rules in a soccer match.

21. The World Cup is played for by soccer playing nations every __ __ __ __ years.

22. The job of a __ __ __ __ __ __ __ is to attack the opposition's goal.

MYSTERY TEAM

___ ___ ___ ___ ___ ___ ___ ___ ___   ___ ___ ___ ___ ___ ___ ___ ___ ___ ___ ___

4. CAROLINE CHISHOLM

Caroline Chisholm was married to an English army officer. The early part of his service was spent in India. In 1838 the family came to settle in New South Wales. Caroline was distressed by what she saw in her new country. She was especially struck by the hopeless position of some of the female immigrants who were often uneducated and unable to find employment.

At first Caroline tried to help individual women, but there were too many for her to deal with on her own. She thought the situation needed action at a government level. Caroline went from official to official until, in 1841, she was given assistance.

She set up a shelter for unemployed girls in an old government building that was no longer in use. After giving them some basic schooling, she found work for them in country areas where there was a shortage of workers. She helped over 700 women in this way.

Caroline saw that Australia's wide – open spaces could provide opportunities for poor people living in crowded cities in England. She also convinced the British government to pay the fare of the wives and families of convicts coming to Australia. By 1846, eleven thousand immigrants had settled in the country due to her efforts. Next she turned her attention to improving the lives of diggers on the goldfields. Most of these people lived in dreadful conditions. She got government assistance to provide wayside shelters for people travelling to the diggings.

Later she moved to Sydney where she founded a girls' school in Newtown. In 1866, wearied by her work, she returned to England. She remained there until her death in 1877. Caroline Chisholm's important contribution to early Australia was recognised by putting her image on the first Australian $5 note.

Immigrant girls land in Sydney.   Emigrants land in Sydney.

A. Write short answers to the questions below.

1. Where did the Chisholms live before coming to Australia? _____

2. When did they come to Australia? _____

3. What were many woman immigrants unable to find? _____

4. What did Caroline start in an old building in 1841? _____

5. Where did many of the women Caroline helped find work? _____

6. What were conditions like in many English cities in Caroline's time? _____

7. Where did she found a girls' school? _____

8. When did Caroline return to England? _____

B. Some words are hiding in CAROLINE CHISHOLM'S name. Find them.

1. a Christmas song __ __ __ __ __   3. you rule it with a ruler __ __ __ __

2. a motor vehicle __ __ __   4. belonging to him __ __ __

C. Find words with these meanings in the information article. The first letter is given.

1. upset d __ __ __ __ __ __ __ __ __ __

2. assistance h __ __ __

3. people who come to a new country to live i __ __ __ __ __ __ __ __ __ __

4. one person i __ __ __ __ __ __ __ __ __ __

5. good chances o __ __ __ __ __ __ __ __ __ __ __ __ __

6. not working u __ __ __ __ __ __ __ __ __

D. Look for an internet image of the old Australian $5 note that featured a picture of Caroline Chisholm. This note circulated from 1967 to 1991. Design your own $5 featuring a famous Australian as its central theme.

	$5
Five Dollar	

Activity

A saint is a person who is especially recognised for their goodness. To the people she helped Caroline must have seemed like a rescuing saint. The words in the word bank all have something to do with saints or sainthood. Match them with their owners or meanings. The highlighted letters spell out the answers to the riddles at the bottom of the activity. Use online resources to find the answers.

> James canonization Vincent George Nicholas patron Jude
> Francis Patrick Mary Christopher Denis Andrew Kilda Gerard
> Ruis Bernadette Elizabeth Abakerazum Aba Mina

1. Saint __ __ __ __ __ __ __ __ __ __ was a bandit and robber who converted to Christianity.

2. Saint __ __ __ __ __ __ is England's patron saint. He is said to have saved people from a dragon.

3. Saint __ __ __ __ __ __ __ was a Roman soldier. He left Caesar's legions to live as a hermit. He was put to death for preaching Christianity.

4. Saint __ __ __ __ __ __ is the patron saint of Scotland, Russia and Greece.

5. Saint __ __ __ __ __ is the patron saint of the city of Paris, France.

6. Saint __ __ __ __ __ is a suburb of Melbourne. It is not clear from where this name comes as there is no saint known who had that name

7. Saint __ __ __ __ __ __ __ de Paul asked wealthy people to give up some of their wealth to help the poor.

RIDDLE 1:

When you know me I am no longer myself. If you don't know me I am something. What am I? I am __ __ __ __ __ __ __ __

8. Saint __ __ __ __ __ __ __ __ is the patron saint of sailors and children.

9. Saint __ __ __ __ MacKillop is the first Australian saint.

10. Saint __ __ __ __ __ __ __ __ __ __ __ is the patron saint of travellers.

11. A __ __ __ __ __ __ saint is a special saint who protects particular places or people.

12. Saint __ __ __ __ is the patron saint of lost causes. People are told to call upon this saint when all else has failed.

RIDDLE 2:
I gallop through the hills, I swerve around mountains. I leap over rivers and wind through the forest. What am I? I am __ __ __ __ __

13. Saint __ __ __ __ __ __ __ __ __ __ was a devout rench girl who discovered the healing waters of Lourdes.

14. __ __ __ __ __ __ __ __ __ __ __ __ is the act of being made a saint.

15. Lorenzo __ __ __ __ is the first saint of the Philippines.

16. Saint __ __ __ __ __ __ Majella is the patron saint of expectant mothers.

17. Saint __ __ __ __ __ __ __ __ __ Ann Seton is the first native born American to be canonized.

18. Saint __ __ __ __ __ __ __, the patron saint of Ireland, is said to have driven the snakes from that country.

19. Saint __ __ __ __ __ is the half brother of Jesus.

20. Saint __ __ __ __ __ __ __ is regarded as the animals' friend.

RIDDLE 3: Who am I? A father's child, a mother's child, yet no-one's son. Who am I? I am the __ __ __ __ __ __ __ __.

This dog is a Saint __ __ __ __ __ __ __.

5. RESCUE WORKERS – PAUL FEATHERSTONE

Thredbo is a village in the snowfields of New South Wales. In winter its population grows as tourists come for skiing holidays. Late at night on 30th July, 1997 there was a terrible landslide.

As part of the village slid down the mountainside it took a building with it. This building, along with tonnes of mud and rocks, slid down and covered another building that was in its path. The rescue operation that followed highlights the bravery and determination of rescue workers.

Many of these workers were unpaid volunteers.

They were in constant danger of the mass of rocks and mud slipping suddenly and burying them alive.

Paul Featherstone was one of the many rescue workers who went to Thredbo to help. He was an ambulance paramedic. Like many others he worked tirelessly searching for survivors.

When Stuart Diver, a ski instructor on the snowfields, was found by Paul he had already been buried under a concrete slab for 65 hours. Paul stayed with him until the young instructor was pulled from the wreckage.

Paul's kind dedication to comforting Stuart reminded everyone of the quiet, caring and often dangerous work that rescue workers do.

A. Write short answers to the questions below.

   1. Why do people come to Thredbo in winter? _____

   2. What terrible disaster happened there on 30th July, 1997? _____

   3. Why was the rescue a dangerous one for the rescue workers? _____

       _____

   4. What was Paul Featherstone's job? _____

   5. Whom did Paul rescue? _____

B. During which season (Spring, Summer, Autumn or Winter) is there the largest number of tourists at Thredbo?

Give a reason for your answer and answer in one or two sentences.

_____

_____

_____

_____

C. Highlight the title that is the most suitable for this text.

   1. Stuart Diver – Hero!

   2. Our Caring Rescue Workers

   3. The Dangers Of Skiing

D. Find words with these meanings in the text. Some letters are given.

   1. courage __ __ __ v __ __ __

   2. peril __ __ __ __ e __

   3. ambulance worker __ __ __ __ __ e __ __ __

   4. devotion to duty __ __ __ __ __ __ __ __ o __

E. Write a letter of thanks from Stuart to Paul thanking him and the other rescue workers for their efforts in the rescue. Write in sentences.

_____

_____

_____

_____

_____

Activity

A. Thredbo is in a mountainous region of Australia. Match each state or territory with its highest mountain below. Choose from the word bank.

Kosciuszko Zeil Bartle Frere Woodroffe
Ossa Bogong Meharry Bimeri

1. New South Wales (2 228 metres) Mount __ __ __ __ __ __ __ __ __ __

2. Victoria (1 986 metres) Mount __ __ __ __ __ __

3. A C T (1 912 metres) __ __ __ __ __ __ Peak

4. Queensland (1 622 metres) Mount __ __ __ __ __ __ __ __ __ __ __

5. Tasmania (1 617 metres) Mount __ __ __ __

6. Northern Territory (1 531) Mount __ __ __ __

7. South Australia (1 435 metres) Mount __ __ __ __ __ __ __ __ __

8. Western Australia (1 253 metres) Mount __ __ __ __ __ __ __

B. Use the internet to choose the correct words from the word bank.

Sagarmatha Chomolungma Himalayas Nepal McLintock

The highest mountain on Australian territory is Mount __ __ __ __ __ __ __ __ __ __ .

It is 3 490 metres tall and is in the Australian Antarctic Territory. The world's highest

mountain is Mount Everest which is 8 840 metres high. It is situated in

___ ___ ___ ___ ___ and is part of the range called the ___ ___ ___ ___ ___ ___ ___ ___ ___. Its

Nepalese name is ___ ___ ___ ___ ___ ___ ___ ___ ___ ___. The people in nearby Tibet call it

___ ___ ___ ___ ___ ___ ___ ___ ___ ___.

C. What Goes With What?

Look at the poem and study its structure.

Mountain Goes with climb.
Lemon Goes With lime.
Snail goes with slime.
Poem goes with rhyme.
But I go with Mum!

Notice there are five lines. The last words of lines 1 to 4 all rhyme. The last line does not. Write your own What Goes With What poem on the lines below. Make at least one line have something to do with mountains.

_____

_____

_____

_____

_____

INDICATORS AND OUTCOMES	**a.** Answers literal questions.
	b. Makes inferences.
	c. Understands the main idea of a text.
	d. Uses context to work out the meaning of words.
	e. Writes a simple personal letter.

6. JOHN FLYNN

Australia is a vast continent. Most people live in towns and cities along its coastline. Much of the country's wealth is generated in remote areas of the inland. People who work and live in these remote areas are at the mercy of what is commonly referred to in Australia as 'the tyranny of distance'.

John Flynn was a Minister of the Presbyterian Church. His work took him to isolated farms and towns in South Australia. Much of his travel there was by camel. As Superintendent of the vast inland region of Central Australia and the Northern Territory he saw how hard life was for people living there. They were hundreds of kilometres from help if they became sick or injured. The roads were poor and travel was difficult.

When, in 1917, a young man called Jimmy Darcy died after falling from a horse, John Flynn knew that something had to be done to stop such tragedies. Jimmy had lived for eleven days after the accident but it took a doctor twelve days to reach him.

Flynn's urgings had already helped to start the Australian Inland Mission in 1913. This allowed nursing hostels and welfare centres to be built within closer reach of where they were needed. But some people were still out of reach of help. With the help of friends and supporters and after many years of hard work Flynn started the Royal Flying Doctor Service in 1928.

Isolated homesteads were given special 'pedal radio' transmitters – receivers so they could send and receive radio messages for help in an emergency. Each remote homestead was provided a standard medical chest with various medicines inside. The people living in remote communities could be given medical advice over the radio. A doctor could be flown to an emergency situation or a patient could be picked up and flown to a hospital if that was necessary. Technology was used to lessen the 'tyranny of distance'.

This service is still very important today. John Flynn's work, in particular the aerial medical services, attracted great interest overseas. He was awarded an OBE (Order of the British Empire) among many honours. He died in 1951 and his ashes were buried in the outback that he loved, beneath a huge boulder near Alice Springs.

A. Write sort answers to these questions.

1. Whereabouts in Australia do most people live?

   _____

2. What was John Flynn's job?

   _____

3. What unusual method of land travel did he often use?

   _____

4. How did Jimmy Darcy die?

   _____

5. What sort of radio did many of the people living in remote areas use to call for emergency help?

   _____

B. How may a flying doctor service have helped prevent Jimmy Darcy's death? Answer in one or two sentences.

   _____

   _____

   _____

   _____

C. Find words with these meanings in the text. Some letters are given.

1. isolated, far away __ E __ __ __ E

2. area __ E __ __ O __

3. sad happenings __ R __ __ __ __ __ __ S

4. farmhouses __ __ M __ __ __ E __ __ __

5. sick person __ __ T __ __ N __

6. large stone __ O __ __ __ E __

D. Highlight the title that is most suitable for this text.

1. Marvels Of Modern Medicine

2. He Worked To Help Others

3. John Flynn – Air Ace

E. Highlight the word that best describes this text?

poem humorous fable information report description adventure novel

F. A tyrant is a cruel ruler (such as a king etc.).

Tyranny is the use of power in a cruel way.
What do you think is meant by **the tyranny of distance**? Write in a sentence(s).

_____

_____

_____

_____

_____

Activity JOHN FLYNN ACTIVITY HEALTH & MEDICAL TERMS

The words in the word bank are all medical or health terms.

Match them with their meanings. The highlighted letters spell out the name of the pledge that doctors swear to uphold when practising medicine. Use an online dictionary to check word meanings. When you have done this complete the puzzle and reveal the doctors' special pledge.

chiropodist anaesthetist dentist dietician paediatrician
dermatologist osteopath antibiotics neurologist acupuncture
psychiatrist orthodontist pathologist respiratory cardiologist
audiologist optometrist herbalist

1. A _ _ _ _ _ _ _ is a doctor who specialises in looking after teeth.

2. A _ _ _ _ _ _ _ _ _ _ _ looks at the behaviour of diseases by studying the blood or body tissue of patients presenting with an illness.

3. A _ _ _ _ _ _ _ _ _ _ _ studies and treats disorders of the nervous system.

4. A ___ ___ ___ ___ ___ ___ ___ ___ ___ ___ treats problems and diseases of people's feet.

5. ___ ___ ___ ___ ___ ___ ___ ___ ___ ___ ___ are medications that are used to kill bacteria.

6. An ___ ___ ___ ___ ___ ___ ___ ___ ___ ___ ___ ___ specialises in testing people's eyes and prescribing corrective lenses.

7. An ___ ___ ___ ___ ___ ___ ___ ___ ___ ___ treats people who are sick or in pain by manipulating the bones and muscles.

8. A ___ ___ ___ ___ ___ ___ ___ ___ ___ ___ ___ illness affects your breathing.

9. A ___ ___ ___ ___ ___ ___ ___ ___ ___ ___ ___ ___ treats heart disorders.

10. A ___ ___ ___ ___ ___ ___ ___ ___ ___ ___ ___ ___ specialises in treating disorders in children.

11. An ___ ___ ___ ___ ___ ___ ___ ___ ___ ___ ___ studies and treats hearing disorders.

12. A ___ ___ ___ ___ ___ ___ ___ ___ ___ ___ ___ ___ diagnoses and treats mental disorders.

13. A ___ ___ ___ ___ ___ ___ ___ ___ ___ is an expert in nutrition (food).

14. ___ ___ ___ ___ ___ ___ ___ ___ ___ ___ ___ treats illnesses by inserting needles into various places in the body.

15. An ___ ___ ___ ___ ___ ___ ___ ___ ___ ___ ___ ___ ___ corrects irregular teeth using braces etc.

16. A ___ ___ ___ ___ ___ ___ ___ ___ ___ ___ ___ ___ ___ ___ treats skin disorders.

17. A ___ ___ ___ ___ ___ ___ ___ ___ ___ ___ uses herbs to make medicines.

18. An ___ ___ ___ ___ ___ ___ ___ ___ ___ ___ ___ administers anaesthetics to patients

The pledge sworn to by doctors is known as:

___ ___ ___   ___ ___ ___ ___ ___ ___ ___ ___ ___ ___ ___   ___ ___ ___ ___ .

INDICATORS AND OUTCOMES	a. answers literal questions
	b. infers, analyses and seeks solutions
	c. uses context to work out the meanings of words
	d. makes inferences
	e. recognises different writing styles and text types
	f. identifies and understands symbolic meeting

On January 1st, 1901, Australia became a federation. This meant that the six self – governing states of New South Wales, Victoria, Queensland, South Australia, Western Australia and Tasmania joined together and became the Commonwealth of Australia. While the states continued to govern in state related matters, the federal government looked after issues concerning the whole nation. It was important that the states, which had formerly been rivals in many things, come together as a united co – operative. An important part of drawing the states together was choosing a flag that emphasized national unity.

In November of 1900 the magazine, The Review Of Reviews Of Australasia, announced a competition to design a national flag. The winner would be given a cash prize of *£50 ($100). Not to be outdone, the authorities announced their own search for a ' Federation Flag ' with a prize of £75 ($150). Not long after, the two groups combined their prizes, offering £75 ($150) each. A tobacco company offered to add £50 ($100) making a total prize of £200 ($400).

When the call for entries closed the judges had the daunting task of selecting one entry from the 32 823 that they received. Some entries even came from other countries.

Many designs featured a variety of Australian wildlife. One entry showed a huge kangaroo with six tails – one for each state. Among all of the entries five that were almost identical were chosen. Their five designers were each given £40 ($80). The designs all showed a Union Jack (the flag of Great Britain) and the Southern Cross on a blue background. Each also featured the larger Federation Star, whose six points represented the six states. A seventh point was added to the Federation Star in 1908. This extra point represented the Australian Territories.

The Australian people slowly warmed to the flag. This altered during the years of World War 1. The sense of patriotism sparked by the war resulted in the flag being warmly accepted as a fine symbol for the young country.

*£ = the symbol for *pounds*. £1 = $2

A. Answer in one sentence.: What is meant by 'Australia became a federation '?

_____

_____

B. Write short answers to the questions below.

1. On which date did Australia become a federation?

_____

2. What was the name of the magazine that ran a competition to design a national flag?

_____

3. What was the first prize in the magazine's competition?

_____

4. What sort of company donated money to the competition run by the authorities?

_____

5. How many entries were received in the competition?

_____

6. What did the six tails on a kangaroo represent on one entry?

_____

7. What did the six points on the Federation Star represent?

_____

8. What did the seventh point that was added in 1908 represent?

_____

C. Inferential Questions.

Sometimes answers to questions do not appear directly in a text. We are able to make conclusions because of other information that is supplied.

EXAMPLE: Consider these sentences in a story:

It had been snowing for five weeks without a stop. Richard was becoming restless having been inside the house for so long. He longed to go outside and play.

Even though we are not told directly, we might conclude that the season was winter. We call this making an inference.

Make inferences then circle **TRUE** or **FALSE** for the sentences below.

1. The Australian flag was used in the Crimean War of 1854   **TRUE   FALSE**

2. There was very little interest in the flag competition.   **TRUE   FALSE**

INDICATORS AND   **a.** writes sentence answers
OUTCOMES   **b.** answers literal questions
                         c. answers inferential questions

ACTIVITY – VOCABULARY

The words in the word bank all have something to do with flags. Use an online dictionary to find their meanings then write the words on the lines provided. The highlighted letters spell out the answers to the riddles below.

staff charge pales saltire Glory vexillology

vexillologist canton Union finial ensign half – mast field

estoile pall June halyard Star fesses hoist

1. A six pointed star which has wavy rays on a flag is called an ___ _ __ __ __ __ __.

2. __ __ __ _ __ __ __ __ __ __ __ is the hobby of collecting and studying flags.

3. America's flag is sometimes called Old ___ _ __ __ __.

4. The background colour of a flag is called its __ __ __ _ __ __.

5. The __ _ __ __ __ Jack is the flag of the United Kingdom.

6. A__ __ __ __ __ __ is any quarter of a flag. Usually it is the top left corner. On Australia's flag it contains the flag of the United Kingdom.

7. An __ __ __ __ __ __ is a national flag displayed on ships and planes of a country's armed forces.

RIDDLE 1: If you say my name I will disappear.

What am I? __ __ __ __ __ __ __ __

8. The correct word for a flag pole is the __ __ __ __ __.

9. A __ __ __ __ is a 'Y' shaped design extending across some flags. The flag of South Africa has one of these.

10. A __ __ __ __ __ __ __ __ __ __ __ __ is someone who collects and studies flags.

11. Wide horizontal bands extending across a flag are called __ __ __ __ __ __. The German flag has these.

12. The __ __ __ __ __ is the edge of a flag that is nearest to the flagpole.

13. A __ __ __ __ __ __ __ is a rope used to raise or lower a flag or sail.

14. A __ __ __ __ __ __ is any emblem that appears by itself on the basic background of a flag. The maple leaf of Canada's flag and the Olympic rings on the Olympic flag are examples.

15. __ __ __ __ 14th is National Flag Day in USA.

16. A __ __ __ __ __ __ __ is a diagonal cross that goes from corner to corner of a flag.

17. The American flag is also called the __ __ __ __ Spangled Banner.

18. A __ __ __ __ __ __ is a decorative fitting on the top of a flagpole.

19. A flag is flown at __ __ __ __ - __ __ __ __ as a sign of mourning.

20. __ __ __ __ __ are wide vertical bands each occupying one third of a flag's area. Italy's flag has these.

RIDDLE 2 : I live in the corner but I travel the world. What am ?

__ __ __ __ __ __ __ __ __ __ __ __ __ __ __ __ __ __

number 11

8. THE DAYS OF THE HAWKERS

How different our shopping habits are today compared to those of earlier times. Using computers to shop online it is now possible for someone living almost anywhere in Australia, no matter how remote, to get in touch with a seller anywhere in the world. People are able to buy goods from distant sellers and have them delivered to the doorstep in less than a week.

Closer to home, everyday shopping is done in large shopping complexes and groceries are bought in supermarkets with a seemingly endless variety of goods available. It wasn't always so.

If you lived in a rural community in the first half of the 20th century, chances are that your house would have been visited by door to door sellers. In the USA they were known as drummers. In Australia we called them hawkers. They were a hardy breed of men (and, less occasionally, women) who travelled, usually on foot, all over the countryside.

They would offer their wares for sale in communities whose shopping was usually done choosing from the limited stock of the nearest grocery shop. For people who lived very far from a township, the trip to the grocer's may have been done once every month or so. A visit from a hawker was often very much welcomed by isolated farm folk.

The wares offered by hawkers were usually small and light – sewing implements, elastic, buttons, combs, matches and mysterious elixirs which, it was claimed, could cure all manner of ailments. These items were commonly wrapped in a square of calico that was neatly folded and carried on the back.

Travelling from farm to farm could mean a journey of several hours as the distance between farm houses was often great, and much of the travel was on Shank's Pony. More times than not, the hawker would be invited to stay and have a chinwag over a cuppa (tea). If it was late in the afternoon an overnight stay was sometimes offered.

Even if money was scarce hawkers were seldom allowed to leave a farmhouse without at least making a small sale. The hawker's run was, in most cases, lengthy. Some regulars would call in about once a year. More frequently they were only ever seen once by their customers. Some managed to scrape together enough money to become successful shop owners and merchants. For many, however, it was a tough and solitary life.

A. Write short answers to the questions below.

1. What special piece of equipment do you need to shop online? _____
_____

2. What sort of items are bought at supermarkets? _____

3. What name was given to door to door sellers in Australia? _____
_____

4. What were they called in USA? _____

5. What form of transport did most hawkers use ? _____

B. Rule lines to link the Australian slang terms with their meanings.

1. *a chinwag*   a social cup of tea

2. *a Wilcannia shower*   the route travelled by a hawker to sell goods

3. *Shanks'pony*   a strong wind blowing from the south

4. *a cuppa*   a dust storm

5. *a run*   the legs

6. *a Southerly Buster*   a friendly talk to pass a bit of time

C. Highlight the title that best suits this text.

1. How To Save Money By Buying From A Hawker

2. The Lonely Life Of The Hawker

3. Australia's First Millionaires

D. Hawkers lived lonely lives and had few comforts. Unjumble the words in the text that describe their difficult, lonely lives.

1. a d y r h __ __ __ __ __

2. s l o t d e a i __ __ __ __ __ __ __ __

3. h o t g u __ __ __ __ __ __

4. o t s l r y a i __ __ __ __ __ __ __ __ __

E. Circle the five items you probably would not buy from a hawker.

1. colour television
2. bobby pins
3. car
4. hamburger
5. ribbon

6. ice cream
7. comb
8. goldfish
9. buttons
10. pencils

Activity – Earning A Living

The words in the word bank all have something to do with work . Match them with their meanings. Highlighted letters spell out the answers to the riddles. Put them in the spaces in the order they occur to solve the riddles.

> wages firm salary commuter pitchman intern redundant
> resign promotion vitae maternity peddler employer
> employee dole trade resume steward tinker apprentice

1. A __ __ __ __ __ __ __ __ is a high pressure seller (usually of small wares).

2. An __ __ __ __ __ __ __ __ __ is a person or company that has people who work for wages or a salary.

3. __ __ __ __ __ are the amounts paid for an hour's work.

4. A __ __ __ __ __ is a skilled manual (done with the hands) job. Examples are plumbers, welders, electricians, mechanics, tilers, plasterers, carpenters etc.

5. The __ __ __ __ is money paid charitably by the state (i.e. government) to people who are not in employment.

6. A __ __ __ __ __ __ is the yearly amount paid to a worker.

7. To quit a job of your own free will is to __ __ __ __ __ __ .

8. and

9. A __ __ __ __ __ __ is a document listing your work qualifications and history. It is also known as a curriculum __ __ __ __ __. You prepare one of these when applying for a job.

10. An __ __ __ __ __ __ __ is someone learning a highly specialised job on the premises to get on the job experience. Trainee doctors working in a hospital and student teachers working in a school are examples.

11. A __ __ __ __ __ __ __ is someone who looks after passengers on a plane or ship.

12. Someone who is given a __ __ __ __ __ __ __ __ __ in their job is given a higher status and more responsibility (and usually more money).

13. An __ __ __ __ __ __ __ __ __ __ is someone who is learning a trade.

14. A __ __ __ __ __ __ is a mender of small items such as pots and pans. **

15. __ __ __ __ __ __ __ __ __ leave is an entitlement of expectant mothers so that they can prepare for the birth and then care for the baby.

16. A __ __ __ __ __ __ __ is a travelling seller of small wares.

17. An __ __ __ __ __ __ __ __ is someone who works for another for wages or a salary.

18. A company or business can also be called a __ __ __ __.

19. You are said to be __ __ __ __ __ __ __ __ __ if your employer no longer needs you.

20. A __ __ __ __ __ __ __ __ is someone who travels a long distance to work every day.

PUZZLES

1. **Q:** Why are waiters good at tennis?
   A: They know __ __ __   __ __   __ __ __ __ .

2. Clarence made millions of dollars every day. In spite of this he lived in a tiny cottage and had many debts. Why do you think this is so?
   A: He __ __ __ __ __ __ at the __ __ __ __ .
   ** also a tinkler

INDICATORS AND OUTCOMES	a. answers literal questions
	b. is able to infer meanings of slang words
	c. understands the main idea of a text
	d. uses context to work out the meaning of words
	e. sees parallels in texts in different contexts

9. ELIZA DONNITHORNE

Eliza Donnithorne was quite the young lady about town. Daughter of the former Governor of the Mint and Judge of the Honorable East India Company of Bengal, Judge James Donnithorne, Eliza was soon to be married to her true love. Arrangements for the wedding had been made. It was to take place in St Stephen's Church, Newtown. The guests would assemble at the family mansion and escort the couple to the church.

Decorations were in place and a magnificent banquet was laid at the tables on the wedding day. To add to the splendour Mother Nature provided beautiful weather on that Spring day in 1854.

The bridesmaids helped Eliza put on her elaborate wedding gown and reported to her of the guests arriving for the splendid occasion. Gowned and looking beautiful, Eliza sat and waited for her fiancé.

The morning passed and still Eliza waited. The mood of the day began to change. The guests began to chatter among themselves as early afternoon turned to mid afternoon and still the bridegroom had not appeared. Those attending to Eliza did their best to console her as she became increasingly anguished. From a joyous occasion the much anticipated event turned to one of sadness and despair. One by one the guests made their apologies and left.

Eliza's fiance was never seen again. Some people believed he had a sudden change of heart. Others said he must have been murdered. It remains one of early Sydney's unsolved mysteries.

As for the stricken bride-to-be, she never lost her sense of grief over the matter. She locked the doors of the big reception room. They remained closed for the rest of her life. The sumptuous feast and the flowers were left to rot in the dark room. Even when they became covered in dust and cobwebs they were not removed. Eliza remained dressed in her wedding gown, hoping to be ready for her lover's return. But it was a reunion that was never to take place. For more than thirty years, until her death in 1886, she waited and hoped.

When the great English author, Charles Dickens, heard of her story he based a character he called Miss Havisham on Eliza. She appears in Dicken's classic novel, Great Expectations. Eliza's headstone can be seen at St Stephen's Cemetery which is also the final resting place of Major Thomas Mitchell and a number of those who lost their lives when the ship, Dunbar, was wrecked.

A. Write short answers below.

   1.   Where was Eliza's wedding to be held? _____

   2.   Why did the guests chatter among themselves as the day went on?

   _____

   3.   Name two things people thought may have happened to the young man.

   (a)_____

   (b)_____

   4.   What had happened to the food that had been laid out?

   _____

   5.   Why did Eliza continue to wear her wedding dress?

   _____

   6.   Which famous author based one of his characters on Eliza? _____

   _____

B. Consider these sentences in a story:

It had been snowing for five weeks without a stop. Richard was becoming restless having been inside the house for so long. He longed to go outside and play. Even though we are not told directly, we might conclude that the season was winter (because it had been snowing for five weeks). We call this making an inference.

Highlight YES or NO to the proposal below and then give a reason for your answer.

Proposal: Eliza's scheduled wedding day was in June 1854.   **YES   NO**

Reason for your answer:

_____

_____

C. PROPER NOUNS

are the special names of people, places, seasons etc. YOU may belong to the group BOYS or GIRLS. The name that your parents gave to you (so people would know what to call you so they didn't mix you up with all the other boys or girls) is a proper noun. Proper nouns always begin with a capital letter. List five proper nouns from the story.

_____

_____

D. Highlight five words that could be used to describe Eliza's feelings as a result of what happened to her.

> despair joy happiness hilarity sadness grief
> power anguish beauty kindness misery

E. Highlight the headline that a newspaper might use to describe this text.

1. Groom Murdered!

2. Mystery Disappearance!

3. Eliza Enjoys Her Big Day!

Eliza lived in a time of rapid expansion for the young colony.

Time lines are used to show events in the order in which they take place. CHRONOLOGY (the order in which things happen) is an important part of the study of history. It helps us understand changes that occur over time.

The timeline below is concerned with the early exploration of Australia.

50 000 BC	Aboriginal people island hop from Java and Sulawesi to mainland Australia. They journey to most parts of the continent.
1400s	Malay fishermen looking for trepang tell stories of coming ashore on a *Great South Land*.
1600s	Dutch spice traders set up the Dutch East India Company in what is modern day Indonesia.
1611	Dutch sea captain, Hendrik Brouwer, follows the wind called the Roaring Forties which made the trip from Holland to the Spice Islands (Indonesia) much faster. This became the preferred route and meant many ships were passing closer to Australia.
1616	Dirk Hartog, captain of the ship *Eendracht*, sails too far east and lands on the desolate coast of WA.
1642	Dutch sea captain, Abel Tasman, lands in Tasmania and, finding no spice bearing plants, declares it to be unsuitable for further exploration by Holland. The Dutch send no more ships to explore the *Great South Land*.
1688 & 1699	English captain, William Dampier makes two journeys to the WA coast. He writes a book about the strange land and raises awareness of it in England.
1770	James Cook explores Australia's east coast and declares it a place worthy of further English exploration
1788	The first fleet of eleven convict ships establishes a penal colony in Sydney Cove. Captain Arthur Philip is Australia's first Governor.
1802-3	Matthew Flinders circumnavigates Australia.
1813	Blaxland, Lawson and Wentworth cross the Blue Mountains, revealing excellent soil and assuring the future of the colony.
1829-30	Charles Sturt solves the *Riddle Of The Rivers*. Rather than flowing into a large inland lake, the rivers were found to enter the ocean in South Australia.

What was the Riddle *Of The Rivers*?

_____

_____

Activity – My Family Timeline

Make your own family time line showing important dates and events concerning your family.

Year	Event (s)

INDICATORS AND OUTCOMES

a. answers direct questions

b. makes inferences

c. identifies grammatical features of a text

d. recognises different character types and traits

e. understands the main idea of a text

10. FREDERICI'S GHOST

The Italian born English opera singer, Frederic Baker, adopted the Italian sounding stage name of *Mr Frederici*. In 1888 he was a member of an opera company which was touring Australia performing the Opera Faust.

The opera tells the story of Doctor Faust, a gifted scholar, who is unhappy with his life. He makes a pact with a demon called Mephistopheles. In exchange for unlimited knowledge he agrees to offer his soul to the demon. In the final scene of the opera Faust must pay his debt and he descends into Hell with Mephistopheles.

The opening Australian performance of this opera took place on the third of March, 1888 at Melbourne's New Princess Theatre.

The opera came to its conclusion and Frederici, who had the part of Mephistopheles, began his descent into Hell with Faust in tow. He descended amid flames through a trapdoor in the stage to the cellar.

As he completed his final note Frederici suffered a heart attack and died. A newspaper report of the time said, 'Mr Frederici, after being laid upon the floor, merely opened his eyes, looked up and closed them again.'

Many of the performers and most of the audience were not aware of what was going on in the cellar. The artists acknowledged the applause of the audience as the body of Frederici lay in the cellar below.

When members of the cast were told what had happened some were shocked. They said that Frederici had been on the stage taking bows with them.

Another baritone replaced Frederici as the opera company continued its tour of Australia without further great incident.

Since that time there have been numerous claims of sightings of a well dressed ghost sitting as if watching a performance on the stage of the New Princess Theatre. On opening nights a seat in the dress circle is left empty for the ghost should he care to come along and watch the performance. It is said to be a good omen if the ghost takes advantage of this offer.

A. Write short answers to the questions below.

1. What was Frederic Baker's stage name? _____

2. What was the name of the opera in which he was performing while touring Australia in 1888?

   _____

3. Which character was he playing in this opera?

   _____

4. What happened when he had sung his last note in the opera?

   _____

5. Why were some of the performers especially shocked when they heard of Mr Frederici's death?

   _____

6. Whereabouts in the New Princess Theatre is a seat still left empty for Mr Frederici to sit on opening nights?

   _____

B. Consider these sentences in a story:

Wendy felt like crying. Try as she would her umbrella would not open. By the time she got to school she would be soaked.

Even though we are not told directly, we might conclude that it was raining (because Wendy was getting wet and she was trying to open her umbrella). We call this *making an inference.*

Highlight YES or NO to the proposal below and then give a reason for your answer.

Mephistopheles does give Doctor Faust the gift of unlimited knowledge.   **YES   NO**

Reason for your answer:

_____

_____

_____

_____

C. Find words with these meanings in the text. Some letters are given.

1. someone who studies __ __ h __ __ a __

2. simply, only __ __ r __ l __

3. a deep male singing voice that is between a bass and a tenor __ a __ __ __ __ n __

4. the first section of seats in an opera house that is usually located above the orchestra __ __ __ __ s __ __ __ c __ __

D. How did the newspaper report the death? Use the exact words written by the paper.

_____

_____

_____

_____

E. ADJECTIVES are words that describe NOUNS. Choose the adjectives in the word bank that best describe each thing below.

appreciative   evil   opening   unexpected

1. The night on which Frederici's ghost is sometimes said to appear. _____

2. the audience _____

3. Mephistopheles _____

4. Frederici's sudden death _____

Activity – Name That Tune

Since Thomas Edison invented the phonograph in 1877 we have been able to record and listen to all the great songs and singers. Before that date we can only read about the great singers. We can now, more than ever, listen to the vast bank of music created by humans by using computer technology. By typing a few words of a song into our computers we can usually do a search that will allow us to find the name of the song.

Match the song name from the title bank to the lyrics. Some artists' names are provided in brackets.

Let Freedom Ring   Blow The Wind Southerly   The Rose Of Tralee
Comin' Thro' The Rye   Wimoweh   God Defend New Zealand
It's a Long Way to Tipperary   Picking Up Pebbles
At The Chocolate Bon Bon Ball   Now Is The Hour   Advance Australia Fair
The Star Spangled Banner

1. E Ihowa Atua, O nga iwi Matou ra (Hayley Westenra)
   Title: _____

2. My country 'tis of thee, sweet land of liberty (Marian Anderson)
   Title: _____

3. In the jungle, the mighty jungle, the lion sleeps tonight (the Tokens,
   Ladysmith Black Mambazo)
   Title: _____

4. The pale moon was rising above the green mountains (John McCormack)
   Title: _____

5. Gin a body kiss a body, need a body cry (Marian Anderson)
   Title: _____

6. Look at the kids on the sandy shore (Matt Flinders)
   Title: _____

7. At twelve o'clock last night, I gently dimmed my light (Leon Redbone)
   Title: _____

8. They told me last night there were ships in the offing (Kathleen Ferrier)
   Title: _____

9. Oh say can you see, by the dawn's early light (Jackie Evancho)
   Title: _____

10. We've golden soil and wealth for toil
    Title: _____

11. Soon you'll be sailing far across the sea (Hayley Westenra)
    Title: _____

12. Up to mighty London came an Irishman one day (John McCormack)
    Title: _____

INDICATORS AND OUTCOMES	a. answers literal questions
	b. makes inferences
	c. uses context to find out the meaning of unknown words
	d. skims a text to locate information
	e. recognises character and other descriptive traits

11. THE TANTANOOLA TIGER

Tantanoola is a small, quiet township in the rural South – East of South Australia. In 1884, while in the Tantanoola district, a Bengal tiger that was with a travelling circus, is said to have escaped. Bengal tigers are known for their size and ferocity.

Following the escape sheep began disappearing from farms in the district. Searches were mounted to try to locate and capture or kill the ferocious beast. People were afraid that the tiger would inevitably turn to humans as its prey. They began to arm themselves. Anyone travelling from a homestead into the township for supplies did so armed with a gun. Gun carrying fathers would escort their children to and from school. A reward was offered to anyone able to capture the tiger – dead or alive. Hunting parties were formed.

Aft.er several months one such hunting party led by experienced bushman and crack shot, Tom Donovan, sighted what looked like a huge wolf voraciously devouring a freshly killed sheep. Donovan quietly positioned himself. He aimed his rifle, took a deep breath and pulled the trigger. The animal dropped, lifeless, to the ground.

It was identified as an Assyrian wolf, not a species that is native to Australia. There were several theories about how this 'tiger' came to be in the district. Some people believed it may have swum ashore from a shipwreck. The animal was embalmed and is still on display at the local hotel.

Cashing in on the 'tiger', the owner renamed his hotel The Tiger Hotel. Things returned to normal for a while. The Bengal tiger was forgotten and local conversation returned to more usual topics such as the weather or the wool prices. For about ten years that appeared to be that.

In the late 1890s a boy, while out riding, claimed that he saw a large, shaggy animal jump over a fence holding a half grown sheep in its jaws. Terrified by what he had seen, he galloped his horse to the nearest farmhouse, declaring to the surprised farmer, 'There's a tiger out there!'

Several hundred sheep had disappeared in the ten years after the death of the first 'tiger'. Could this be its mate? Perhaps there was more than one Assyrian wolf in the district. Or perhaps the Assyrian wolf had mated with native wild dogs to breed some sort of super predator. Maybe it was the Bengal tiger that had escaped from the circus in 1884. The number of sheep disappearing again began to rise.

Tales of a new Tantanoola tiger spread like wildfire through the district. Once again hunting and trapping parties set out to find this new threat. The wider the story spread the greater the number of sheep disappeared. But year by year the cunning 'tiger' avoided its pursuers. In one week in November 1910 more than 150 sheep went missing from different flocks. Despite most locals being convinced that the raids on flocks of sheep were the work of the 'tiger', some authorities began to believe it may have been caused by human hands.

In January, 1911, a trio of local sharpshooters, Frank Osborne and the Burchard brothers came upon a site in isolated swampland that looked like a corral. Lying all around were piles of bones. They rode into town and told the local constable of their find. He told them to tell no-one of their discovery. A few days later a swaggie came to Tantanoola. He went to the hotel where he chatted and had some drinks with a number of locals. He then left as quickly as he had appeared. A few days later he returned, but he was not a swaggie this time. He walked up to Robert Charles Edmondson, a local identity and arrested him on a charge of sheep stealing. Together with a partner, who later gave evidence against him, Edmondson had been stealing the sheep, skinning them and selling their hides in Adelaide. The police witness said that on some nights they would steal and skin twenty sheep. This would make them £5 ($10) a day, a sizeable amount at that time.

Edmondson was imprisoned for six years. The disappearances of sheep ceased. The Tantanoola tiger had taken its last victim.

COMPREHENSION

A. Write short answers below.

1. In which Australian state is Tantanoola? _____

2. What is said to have escaped from a circus travelling near Tantanoola in 1884?

   _____

3. What began disappearing in the area following this escape?

   _____

4. What were people afraid of the creature turning to as prey?

   _____

5. What did Tom Donovan shoot? _____

6. How did this creature come be in the Tantanoola district?

   _____

7. Where is this embalmed 'tiger' still on display? _____

8. What did the boy who was out riding in the 1890s think he saw?

   _____

9. How many sheep went missing in one week of November 1910? _____

10. What did Frank Osborne and the Burchard brothers come across in January, 1911?

    _____

11. What was the policeman who arrested Edmondson disguised as?

    _____

12. What was Edmondson charged with?

    _____

    _____

    _____

B. Find words with these meanings in the text. Some letters are given.

1. fierce __ __ __ o __ __ o __ __

2. groups __ a __ t __ __ __

3. an animal that hunts, kills and eats other animals __ r __ __ __ t __ __

4. eating greedily __ e __ __ __ __ __ n __

5. chasers __ __ __ s __ e __ __

6. an enclosure or pen for sheep, horses, cattle etc. __ __ r __ a __

7. a labourer who carries his personal possessions in a pack or swag while travelling about in search of work __ __ a __ __ __ e

8. large __ __ z __ __ b __ __ __

C. Number the events in the order they took place. The first one is done.

1. Frank Osborne and the Burchard brothers came upon huge piles of bones in some swampland near Tantanoola. __4__

2. Robert Edmondson was arrested and charged with sheep stealing. _____

3. A Bengal tiger escaped from a circus near Tantanoola. _____

4. A boy who was out riding saw a large shaggy animal with a half grown sheep in its jaws. ____

5. Tom Donovan shot an Assyrian wolf. _____

ACTIVITY

The words in the word bank all have something to do with cats. Match them with their meanings. The highlighted letters spell out the answers to the riddles at the bottom of the activity. Use online resources to find the answers.

tongue feline mouser panther tabby kitten veterinarian lynx tom felidae licks lion meowing mewing manx puma Persian leopard cheetah purr

1. A__ __ __ __ __ __ __ __ is a black variant of a number of members of the cat family.

2. A __ __ __ __ __ is also known as a cougar.

3. The sound that a contented cat makes is its __ __ __ __.

4. A sick cat should be taken to a __ __ __ __ __ __ __ __ __ __ __ __.

5. The sound a young cat makes is its __ __ __ __ __.

6. A__ __ __ __ __ __ cat has very long hair.

7. A cat__ __ __ __ __ its hair to keep it neatly groomed.

8. Any member of the cat family is a __ __ __ __ __ __.

RIDDLE 1: What is a cat's favourite colour? Answer: __ __ __ __ __ __ __ __

9. A __ __ __ __ __ cat is grey or brown and mottled with dark stripes.

10. A__ __ __ __ __ __ __ is known for its spotted hide.

11. The__ __ __ __ is said to be the king of beasts.

12. The sound an adult cat makes is its __ __ __ __ __ __ __.

13. A __ __ __ __ is a yellowish brown wildcat with a short tail and tufted ears. It is found in the northern regions of America, Asia and Europe.

14. Reaching speeds of up to 104 kilometres per hour, the__ __ __ __ __ __ __ is the fastest land animal.

15. The __ __ __ __ cat is native to the Isle Of Mann. It has no tail.

16. If a cat likes you it will often lick you with its rough__ __ __ __ __ __.

RIDDLE 2: What kind of cat likes ten pin bowling?
Answer: __ __ __ __ __   __ __ __

17. A__ __ __ __ __ __ is a baby cat (or rabbit).

18. The cat family is known as the __ __ __ __ __ __ __.

19. A male cat is called a __ __ __.

20. Any animal that catches mice is a __ __ __ __ __ __.

RIDDLE 3: What do kittens become when they finish medical school?
Answer: first aid __ __ __ __

INDICATORS AND OUTCOMES

a. answers literal questions

b. uses context to work out the meaning of words

c. can sequence events in a text

12. AUSTRALIAN ECCENTRICS #1 THE FLYING PIEMAN

An eccentric is a person who is different from most other people. Sometimes they are referred to as being non-conformists or originals. William Francis King, who came to be known as The Flying Pieman was such a person. He thought physical fitness was more important than anything else.

Born in London in 1807, his restless nature brought him to Sydney in 1829. Among numerous jobs he was a barman at the Hope And Anchor Tavern on the corner of King and Pitt Streets, Sydney. (If you go there today you will see huge multi storey office buildings.) He added to his earnings by making and selling pies near Hyde Park and at Circular Quay. His cry of, 'Pies! Hot pies! Kidney, pork, apple and mutton pies! Hot pies!' became familiar to the people of the area. As a result of this he came to be known as The Flying Pieman.

He would offer his pies to passengers at the quay who were boarding the steamer to Parramatta. When it departed he would run the 30 kilometres to Parramatta and offer any unsold pies to the same passengers as they disembarked, having reached their destination.

Saddened by an unsuccessful love affair, he found the best way of calming his mind was by going on very long walks. Although he had always been interested he had been unaware that he was so outstandingly good at them. He began racing long distances against coaches, ferries or the clock. He made money by successfully betting on himself.

Twice he beat the mail coach from Windsor to Sydney, a distance of 50 kilometres. Easily recognisable, his usual dress was a blue jacket, bright red trousers and an old top hat with coloured streamers attached to it.

Word of his extraordinary talent soon spread and no-one was prepared to gamble against him. Without money he soon became homeless and destitute. He was taken in by the Liverpool Asylum. He spent the remainder of his life there and died in 1873, aged 66 years. It was a sad ending for a man whose gentle sense of fun had brought happiness to so many.

COMPREHENSION

A. Write shorts answers below.

1. What is an *eccentric*?

2. List two other names that can be used to refer to an eccentric.

3. What was the real name of the man who came to be known as The Flying Pieman?

4. What did the Pieman think was the most important thing in life?

5. Where and in which year was he born?

6. When did the Pieman come to Sydney?

7. At which hotel did he work as a barman?

8. What did he make and sell to add to his income?

9. What was his famous call as he sold his pies?

10. To the passengers of which steamer did he sell his pies?

11. How far did he have to run to meet the steamer's disembarking passengers?

12. What caused him great sadness?

13. What did he find was the best way to calm his mind?

14. What sorts of vehicles did he race? (name two)

_____

15. What is meant by racing against the clock

_____

16. How did he make money from the races he contested?

_____

17. Over what distance did he race the Windsor to Sydney mail coach?

_____

18. How was he usually dressed when racing?

_____

19. When and where did he die?

_____

20. How was he remembered?

_____

B. Find words with these meanings in the text. Some letters are given?

1. money made by working __ __ __ n __ n __ __

2. meat of a sheep __ __ t __ o __

3. organ that filters the blood __ __ d __ e __

4. meat of a pig __ o __ __ __

5. about __ __ __ __ __ __ __ m __ t __ __ __

6. left __ __ __ __ r __ e __

7. got off a boat __ __ __ __ __ b __ __ k __ __

8. well known __ __ __ i __ __ a __

9. beyond normal __ __ __ __ __ o __ __ __ n __ __ __

10. suffering extreme poverty __ __ __ __ __ __ t __ t __

INDICATORS & OUTCOMES	**a.** answers literal questions (1–14, 16–20)
	b. uses context to work out the meaning of figurative language (Q. 15)
	c. uses context to find out the meaning of words

ENRICHMENT ACTIVITY

A. Choose and highlight the word from each pair that best describes the Flying Pieman

restless or composed   lazy or hardworking   relaxed or busy

unusual or uninteresting   emotional or steady

B. Among the pies sold by the pieman were kidney, pork and mutton pies.

Next to the meats below write the animals they come from. Use the internet to research your answers.

1. pork   _____

2. mutton   _____

3. beef   _____

4. venison   _____

5. poultry   _____

6. veal   _____

C. The pieman's street cry was: 'Pies! Hot pies! Kidney, pork, apple and mutton pies! Hot pies!' In his time it was very common practice for street sellers to have a cry to attract customers.

Make up your own street cry and write it on the lines below. Practise it on your friends.

_____

_____

_____

D. The pieman is described in the following way:

'Easily recognisable, his usual dress was a blue jacket, bright red trousers and an old top hat with coloured streamers attached to it. Use this description to guide you draw and colour a picture of him racing along at high speed.

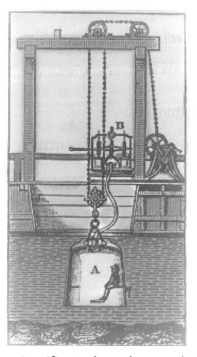

Henry Grien came to Australia from Switzerland in the 1870s. He was a convincing liar. Towards the end of his life he admitted this. At this time he was touring England and South Africa with a stage play billing himself as The Greatest Liar on Earth. He was a man who could convince people that the ridiculous was possible. Gullible investors would trip over themselves to buy into his worthless schemes. Invariably they lost all of their money.

One of his earliest inventions was a diving bell. He offered this for sale in 1896. Some Sydney investors paid him handsomely for the rights to his creation. When it was tried out the two men inside it drowned.

Grien fled to New Zealand and then England to escape police inquiries about his dubious activities. While in England his smooth talking managed to convince the owners of the reputable World Wide Magazine that he had a background in scientific study and research. He did this using the name Louis De Rougemont.

He wrote imaginative accounts of adventures in Australia. These accounts bore the long winded title The Adventures Of Louis De Rougemont As Told By Himself. In these tales he wrote of a series of close brushes with death among cannibalistic natives in Australia's north east.

He also described wild adventures riding on the backs of dolphins and turtles as they swam through the water.

But when he wrote telling of 'a flight of wombats rising in the dusk', people began questioning his articles.

The final straw was when he told his readers of flying pigs that lived in deep underground burrows. That stretched the bounds of what was believable too far.

He was told by his publishers that his services would no longer be required. Henry Grien was penniless when he died in a Kensington, London workhouse in 1921.

COMPREHENSION

A. Write short answers below.

1. From which country did Henry Grien come to Australia? _____

2. Which two countries did Grien tour? _____

3. What title did he give himself when he toured? _____

4. What invention did Grien offer for sale in 1896? _____

5. What happened to the two men inside this invention?

_____

6. Which well respected magazine did he write for?

_____

7. Under what name did he write articles for this magazine?

_____

8. What name did he give to his imaginary adventures?

_____

9. Where did he say he encountered cannibals? _____

10. On the backs of which animals did he claim to ride? _____

11. What was unusual about Grien's wombats and pigs?

_____

12. Where did his pigs supposedly live? _____

13. Where did Grien die? _____

14. What might lead you to think that 'crime does not pay 'when you read Grien's life story?

_____

B. Find words with these meanings in the text. Some letters are given.

1. believable __ __ n __ __ __ c __ __ __

2. easily tricked __ __ __ __ __ b __ e

3. bell shaped vessel used for underwater work; it is open at the bottom and supplied with pressurised air __ __ v __ __ __ __ e __ __

4. honourable __ __ p __ __ __ b __ __

5. the period of time at the end of the day just before it becomes dark __ __ __ __

ACTIVITY

HENRY GRIEN HOAXES, FRAUDS & CHARLATANS

The words in the word bank all have something to do with dishonesty and trickery. Match them with their meanings. The highlighted letters spell out the name of the supposed supernatural creature at the bottom of the activity. Use an online dictionary and the internet to check meanings or the names linked to some of the schemes.

WAR OF THE WORLDS METRIC GULLIBLE SPAGHETTI FRAUD GRIFTER
ICEBERG PILTDOWN NAILS MARY TOFT SUCKER RING-IN CLEVER HANS
FORGERY CHEAT FIJI MERMAID PLATYPUS COUNTERFEIT CARABOO
SMELLOVISION

1. A hoax broadcast by Britain's BBC on April Fool's Day in 1957 showed Swiss farmers harvesting _ _ _ _ _ _ _ _ _ from trees. Many people were 'taken in' by this hoax.

2. In the 1940s an Australian hoaxer advertised in the newspaper that if people sent him an amount of money he would reveal the secret method used by people who had become rich and successful. For their money they were sent a sheet of paper with the single word '_ _ _ _ _' written on it.

3. A _ _ _ _ _ _ _ is an American slang term for someone who tricks people into giving them money.

4. Princess _ _ _ _ _ _ _ was the name used by a servant girl who masqueraded as an exotic princess in the English village of Almondsbury. She was found in April of 1817, dressed in unusual clothes, wandering the streets of the village and speaking in her own made up language.

5. The _ _ _ _ _ _ _ _ Man was a hoax perpetrated by some British students in 1912. Combining a human skull with the jawbone of an orang – utan they made their own 'missing link'.

6. In 1938 an American radio broadcast version of H G Wells' famous science fiction story _ _ _ _ _ _ _ _ _ _ _ _ _ _ _ caused mass panic. People thought that the Earth really was being invaded by aliens from Mars.

7. A _ _ _ _ _ _ _ _ _ _ _ _ is a copy. It is the term mainly used to describe copies of money, especially bank notes.

8. P T BARNUM, called himself the greatest showman on Earth. He used the head and chest of a monkey combined with the tail of a large fish to create a display he called the _ _ _ _ _ _ _ _ _ _ _.

9. Sometimes young people beginning in a job are send on prank errands asking for such non existent things as a long wait, a skyhook, a bucket of steam or rubber _ _ _ _ _.

10. On 1st April, 1978, what looked like an _ _ _ _ _ _ _ was towed into Sydney Harbour. It was the idea of businessman, Dick Smith. He said he would cut it into cubes and sell it to Sydneysiders at ten cents a cube. He claimed that a cube added to any drink would improve its flavour. People looked on in awe. A passing April shower revealed the iceberg to be a combination of

shaving cream and fire fighting foam towed by a barge. In a short time the 'iceberg' surrendered to the shower and dissolved.

11. _ _ _ _ _ _ _ _ _ was a horse whose owner claimed could solve difficult mathematical problems and tap out the answer with his hoof. His owner had trained him to stop tapping by using subtle signals when the answer was reached. People didn't notice these signals believing the horse had worked out the answer himself.

12. On April 1st, 1975, Australian current affairs program, This Day Tonight, announced that Australia would soon convert to _ _ _ _ _ _ time. An hour would consist of 100 minutes and each minute of 100 seconds. It was, of course, an April Fool's Day hoax.

INDICATORS & OUTCOMES	a. answers literal questions 1–10, 12 and 13
	b. answers inferential questions 11 and 14
	c. uses context to find the meaning of words

HENRY GRIEN HOAXES, FRAUDS & CHARLATANS (2)

13. A _ _ _ _ _ _ _ is a copy of something made to deceive others.

14. _ _ _ _ _ _ _ _ was an Englishwoman who, in 1726, fooled some prominent doctors into believing she had given birth to rabbits.

15. When a stuffed _ _ _ _ _ _ _ _ was sent to England in the early days of Australia's European colonisation many people thought it was a hoax.

16. Someone who is easily fooled is said to be _ _ _ _ _ _ _ _.

17. A _ _ _ _ _ is an act of trickery used for unlawful gain.

18. When one racehorse is secretly substituted for another it is said to be a _ _ _ _ - _ _.

19. Legendary showman, P T Barnum was confident that he could fool anyone. He is famous for saying, 'There's a _ _ _ _ _ _ born every minute.'

20. On April Fool's Day, 1965, the BBC broadcast that it had developed technology that allowed it to send smells through to the homes of television viewers. A supposed scientist claimed to have transmitted the aromas of coffee beans and onions. People were asked to telephone in if the aromas were reaching their homes. Many did that. He called his invention _ _ _ _ _ _ _ _ _ _ _ _ _.

Puzzle

In 1917 two young cousins, Elsie Wright and Frances Griffiths, took some photographs which, when developed looked like dancing fairies. They were shown to Sir Arthur Conan Doyle, the author who created the character, Sherlock Holmes. Doyle thought the pictures may have been authentic. The girls in the pictures came to be known as

_ _ _ _ _   _ _ _ _ _ _ _ _ _ _   _ _ _ _ _ _ _ _

14. SAMMY COX
AUSTRALIAN ECCENTRICS #3
AN EXTRAORDINARY LIFE

The man in the picture on this page looks modest and undistinguished. It is, however, the photograph of a man who had a remarkable life. The man's name is Sammy Cox and the picture was taken well after he had reached one hundred years of age.

Sammy Cox was born Samuel Emmanuel Jarvis in November, 1773.

His father, a wealthy English squire (landowner), died when he fell from a horse while fox hunting in 1789. The sixteen year old Sammy was put into the care of his uncle, the sea captain, John Jarvis.

In an effort to take Sammy's mind off this sad event Captain Jarvis took him on a whale hunting expedition in the waters around northern Tasmania.

The sailors manning the ship were mischievous with young Sammy. They teased him with stories that his uncle was going to abandon him on a deserted island. The reason for this, they told the teenager, was so that Captain Jarvis could inherit the property left to Sammy. Frightened by these stories, Sammy decided to escape from his uncle by hiding in the bush.

Because they could not find him, his uncle and the crew thought that he must have met with a dreadful accident. After searching for a few days they sailed away without him.

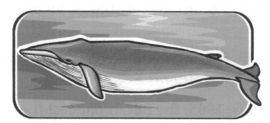

Poor Sammy must have been terrified. Luckily for him some aborigines befriended him and took him in as one of their tribe. They treated him kindly and he lived with them until European settlement came to the Launceston district in 1806.

He left his aboriginal friends and was adopted by a family called Cox and took on their name.

Sammy worked as a gardener and handyman for his adopted family for many years. When they passed away he continued doing this sort of work in the district around Launceston for another 50 years.

Sammy died in June, 1891 at the incredible age of 117 years. His life story was so unusual that some people question whether everything that Sammy said was truthful.

A. Write short answers below.

1. When was Sammy Cox born? _____

2. What tragic event happened to his father when Sammy was sixteen years old?

_____

3. Into whose care was Sammy put after this tragedy?

_____

4. What was the occupation of John Jarvis?

_____

5. What did John Jarvis decide might take Sammy's mind off his father's death?

_____

6. What did the sailors tell Sammy his uncle planned to do to him?

_____

7. Where did Sammy hide? _____

8. What did the crew and Sammy's uncle think must have happened to him?

_____

9. What did they do after searching for Sammy for a few days?

_____

10. Who befriended Sammy? _____

11. What did they allow him to become?

_____

12. When did European settlement come to Launceston?

_____

13. What was the name of the family that adopted Sammy?

_____

14. What was Sammy's job with this family?

_____

15. When did Sammy die?

_____

16. How old was he when he died?

_____

B. Find words with these meanings in the text. Some letters are given.

1. rich __ __ a __ __ h __

2. uninhabited __ __ __ __ r __ e __

3. journey taken by a group of people for a particular reason __ x __ __ __ __ __ __ n

4. terrible __ __ e __ __ f __ __

5. amazing __ __ __ __ h __ e

C. Two of the headlines below could not be written. Highlight them and give a reason why you chose one of them.

1. SAMMY COX FOUND BY NEW SETTLERS IN LAUNCESTON!!!

2. SAMMY COX TO ACCOMPANY UNCLE ON WHALING TRIP!!!

3. SQUIRE JARVIS KILLED IN FOX HUNT!!!!

I chose _____ because _____

_____

_____

_____

SAMMY COX AUSTRALIAN ECCENTRICS #3 ENRICHMENT

Sammy sat, somewhere between emotionless and panic. A million things raced through his mind at once. Underlining it, however, was the stunning realisation – he was lost! From the comfort of his bedroom back in England, being marooned on a tropical island seemed to be the grandest thing ever. But, being in that position, really lost and alone – that was vastly different.

A. The paragraph above may have described Sammy's feelings when he realised he was lost. Extend the paragraph mentioning other things that may have raced through his mind. Use the lines below.

_____

_____

_____

_____

_____

_____

But all of these thoughts would have to wait – no long lost pirates' treasures, no fabulous exotic animals. No, not now at any rate. The first thing he had to do was find a safe place to sleep!

B. Someone from Tasmania is called a Tasmanian. Sometime the slang term *Taswegian* is used. Match the slang terms with their states or territories. Use the internet to do your research.

1. A Croweater comes from the state, _____

2. A Sandgroper comes from the state, _____

3. A Bananabender comes from _____

4. A Top Ender comes from the northern part of the_____

C. Sammy's uncle took him on a whale hunting expedition. A hunted whale will dive to avoid hunters. Unlike a fish, however, the whale must eventually come to the surface again to breathe. Why is this so? Use the internet to help you with your research.

_____

_____

D. The picture shows a unicorn.

This mythological creature is believed to be based on sailors' descriptions of narwhals, members of the same family as whales. Use an image search on your computer to find a picture of a narwhal. Draw a picture of a narwhal using your researched image as a model.

INDICATORS & OUTCOMES	**a.** answers literal questions
	b. can use context to find out the meaning of words
	c. analyses text and makes logical inferences

Irishman, Francis de Groot, came to Australia in 1910. To casual observers he seemed to be a quite unremarkable man. He made a modest living buying and selling antiques in Sydney.

Mr de Groot, however, was a fiercely loyal supporter of English royalty. He belonged to an organisation of like – minded people that was known as the *New Guard*.

In 1932 Mr de Groot's love of the royal family was to bring him from obscurity to prominence.

The Premier of New South Wales at that time was the staunch anti – royalist, Jack Lang. Lang made no secret of the fact that Australia should break away from England and the royal family.

De Groot was angry when he learnt that Lang was to cut the ceremonial ribbon to open Sydney's engineering marvel, the Sydney Harbour Bridge. He believed that this was a job that should be done by a representative of the English crown. He believed that the Governor General was the perfect choice.

On the day of the bridge's opening Francis de Groot put on his New Guard uniform. When he was quite near the ceremonial proceedings he mounted his horse and charged through the crowd with his sword raised. Coming to the ribbon he cut it with his sword. He had beaten Lang to the punch!

As the sliced through the ribbon he shouted, 'On behalf of the decent, loyal citizens of New South Wales I declare this bridge open!'

Francis de Groot

He was arrested and fined for this and eventually returned to Ireland where he lived quietly for the rest of his life.

COMPREHENSION

A. Write short answers below.

1. In which country did Francis de Groot live before coming to Australia?

   _____

2. In which year did he come to Australia? _____

3. How did he make a living? _____

4. Of whom was de Groot a supporter? _____

5. To which group did he belong? _____

6. Who was NSW Premier in 1932? _____

7. What was Lang going to cut to open the Sydney Harbour Bridge?

_____

8. Whom did de Groot think should cut the ribbon?

_____

9. What did de Groot use to cut the ribbon?

_____

10. What did de Groot shout as he cut the ribbon? _____

11. What was his punishment for cutting the ribbon? _____

12. In which country did Francis de Groot die? _____

B. Find words with these meanings in the text. Some letters are given.

1. small __ __ d __ s __

2. members of the royal family __ __ y __ __ t __

3. people who think the same are this __ __ k __ - __ __ __ d __ __

4. the state of not being well known __ __ s __ __ __ __ t __

5. the state of being well known __ __ __ m __ __ __ n __ __

6. showing strong belief in something __ t __ u __ __ __

C. In the text it says de Groot had 'beaten Lang to the punch.' Write what this means in your own words.

_____

_____

_____

INDICATORS & OUTCOMES	**a.** answers literal questions
	b. can use context to work out the meaning of words
	c. recognises imagery and is aware of it as a literary device

AUSTRALIAN ECCENTRICS 1 - 4

Sydney Harbour Bridge

16. ELIZA FRASER'S EXTRAORDINARY ORDEAL

Lying almost three hundred kilometres north east of Brisbane is the world's largest sand island. Today the island is a tourist attraction. People from all over the world visit to go on whale and dolphin watching tours and to view the region's other natural wonders. Named K'gari by the local Butchulla Aboriginal people and Great Sandy Island by early European visitors, the island was renamed Fraser Island after James Fraser, Captain of the ship, Stirling Castle, and his wife, Eliza. The Butchulla name means Paradise. To the people on board the Stirling Castle, however, it was far from being a paradise.

In 1836 wild seas caused the ship to founder. Seventeen crew and passengers managed to scramble on board lifeboats before the ship went down. When the winds eventually receded the survivors decided that their best chance of reaching safety was to set sail southwards in the hope of reaching the penal settlement at Moreton Bay (now Brisbane). While they were in the lifeboats the pregnant Eliza gave birth but the child died on the same day.

Hopping onto islands and reefs for about three weeks to gather what they could to eat, they soon came to what was then called Great Sandy Island.

The exhausted castaways traded clothes and tomahawks with some of the Aboriginal people to whom the island was home. Having had little contact with Europeans, the Aborigines believed them to be ghosts – the ghosts of an enemy tribe. They overpowered

the strange visitors and made them their slaves. Mrs Fraser later told of how she had watched as her husband was beaten and finally speared to death by their captors. For several months she was made a slave to the women of the tribe.

It was at the time of her enslavement that a group of Aborigines from another tribe living on Great Sandy Island came to visit John Graham, a convict friend. He was finishing his prison term at Moreton Bay. He had befriended these Aborigines after escaping from captivity and hiding on Great Sandy Island. The natives believed that he, too was a ghost, but the ghost of a past member of their tribe, and, therefore, friendly. After some time he had been recaptured by penal authorities who returned him to Moreton Bay to complete his prison term.

The Aborigines told Graham about the 'white ghosts' living with the rival tribe on Great Sandy Island.

When informed of this by Graham, the head of the penal settlement sent a party to search for the remaining survivors. When the rescue party came into contact with the Aborigines they traded goods in exchange for their 'slaves', saying that they were relatives.

Only a few of the original survivors of the Stirling Castle survived the ordeal. Two men had made up their minds to try their luck swimming from the island. Their horrified companions looked on helplessly as a huge shark appeared and devoured them both.

On her return journey to England on a ship called The Mediterranean Packet Eliza married the ship's captain, Alexander John Greene. She travelled to various places giving paid talks about her ordeal. What some people believed to be a sensationalized account of what had happened was recalled in a book called A Mother's Offering To Her Children, written in 1841 by Charlotte Barton. Eliza was never identified in the book which was written in the form of a mother talking in an instructional dialogue to her four children. It is regarded as the first Australian book written for children.

Eliza Fraser died in 1858 when she was involved in a carriage accident in Melbourne. Thus ended a life seemingly plagued by a procession of unwanted sensational events.

COMPREHENSION

A. Write short answers below.

1. Whereabouts is Fraser Island in relation to Brisbane? _____

2. Why do many tourists go there? _____

3. What name do the Butchulla aborigines give to the island? _____

4. What does this name mean in English? _____

5. Which ship was captain Fraser in charge of? _____

6. How many people managed to scramble aboard the lifeboats?

_____

7. In which year did this happen? _____

8. What happened to Elisa's newborn baby ?

_____

9. Towards which penal settlement did they decide to sail?

_____

10. What was the name of Fraser Island in 1836?

_____

11. What did the aboriginals think the castaways were?

_____

12. How did Captain Fraser die?

_____

13. What was the name of the convict who had befriended the other tribe on the island?

_____

14. What did these aborigines call the castaways?

_____

15. What happened to the two men who tried to swim away from the island?

_____

16. On which ship did Eliza make her return journey to England?

_____

17. Whom did she marry on this return voyage ?

_____

18. In which early children's book are Eliza's adventures mentioned?

_____

19. Who wrote this book?

_____

20. How did Eliza die?

_____

B. Find words with these meanings in the text. Some letters are given.

1. a perfect place __ __ __ a __ __ s __

2. to fill with water and sink __ o __ __ d __ __

3. people who are stranded in a remote place as a result of shipwreck etc. __ __ s __ __ __ __ y __

A. Perhaps the best known shipwreck story is **Robinson Crusoe** published in 1719. Who is the author of this book? Use the internet to find the answer._____

B. A character similar to Eliza is mentioned in the book **A Mother's Offering To Her Children.**

This is believed to be regarded as the first Australian book written for children. Do an internet search to find the authors of the children's books below. The names are also listed in the word bank. Cross reference them with the names found on the internet.

> **Margaret Mahy Enid Blyton Jeff Brown Roald Dahl JRR Tolkien Randolph Stow Beatrix Potter Jeff Kinney Hans Christian Andersen Anna Sewell**

1. *Black Beauty* was written by _____
2. *The Great White Man-Eating Shark* was written by _____
3. *The Ugly Duckling* was written by _____
4. *The Hobbit* was written by _____
5. *Noddy Goes To Toyland* was written by _____
6. *The Diary Of A Wimpy Kid* was written by _____
7. *Midnite* was written by _____
8. *The Tale Of Peter Rabbit* was written by _____
9. *The Twits* was written by _____
10. *Flat Stanley* was written by _____

C. In Eliza Fraser's time the aborigines were semi nomadic. They were described as being **hunter-gatherers ..In a sentence tell what you think is meant by the term hunter-gatherer.**

_____

_____

D. How do you think the aborigines felt about the strange new visitors? Write one good thing and one bad thing from their point of view.

_____

_____

17. P G TAYLOR

From an early age flying fascinated P G Taylor. Not only did he become known as a brilliant pioneering airman, but he was to gain the reputation as a man of great courage as a result of an extraordinary incident.

Patrick Gordon Taylor was born in Sydney in 1896. When the opportunity came to join the Royal Flying Corps during World War I (1914–1918) he took it without hesitation. He was awarded the Military Cross for bravery during the war.

After the conflict he served as a pilot for one of this country's pioneering airlines, Australian National Airways. This was at a time when aviators dominated the headlines of newspapers because of their achievements. Air races were held and aviators were constantly trying to break records for the time taken to make long distance flights.

The record for a flight from England to Australia had progressively fallen. From Keith Smith's original record of 15 days in 1928 it was lowered by Bert Hinkler in 1930 (10 days), Charles Kingsford Smith in 1933 (7 days) and again by Kingsford Smith in 1934 (2 days and 23 hours) .

Taylor was an associate of Kingsford Smith, Australia's best known aviator.

In 1935 he and 'Smithy' were involved in flying the aircraft Lady Southern Cross from Sydney to New Zealand to deliver the Royal Jubilee mail.

The Jubilee was to celebrate King George V's 25th year as King of England.

While flying across the Tasman Sea, one of the aeroplane's engines failed. They decided to turn back to Australia. As they began the return flight the remaining engine started losing oil. If that engine failed the aeroplane would surely have come down in the sea.

Showing incredible courage , Taylor climbed onto the aircraft's wing, drained some oil from the failed engine and transferred it to the one that was still working. He did this five times in all and, because of his bravery, they were able to land the plane safely on Australian soil.

When the story became known Taylor's courageous actions were acclaimed. He received a bravery award called the George medal.

King George V

His love of flying continued throughout his life. He, once again, saw military service in the RAF (Royal Air Force) during World War II (1939–1945). He wrote eight books about flying, was knighted (given the title of 'Sir') in 1954, and died in 1966.

P.G. TAYLOR CROSSWORD

Across

3. This failed on the flight to New Zealand.
9. P.G. Taylor had to climb onto this to change the oil.
10. Kingsford Smith's aeroplane was called 'Lady Southern_____'.
14. Aeroplanes fly up in the ___.
15. You drive a car on this.
16. A male sheep.
17. A weapon that shoots bullets.
18. They were flying over the Tasman___.
20. Good, _____, best.
23. An animal doctor.
24. Five fingers make one of these.
25. Without oil the engine would get too ____.
26. Short for Peter.
27. You measure and rule lines with one of these.
30. A pilot.
31. What the engine was losing.
33. Short for Neville.
34. You have these when you sleep.
36. Abbreviation for 'year'.
38. P.G. Taylor wrote this number of books about flying.
39. Another word for engine.

Down

1. Initials of Royal Flying Corps.
2. P.G. Taylor received this medal for bravery.
4. North-west (initials).
5. Initials for American soldier: 'General Infantryman'
6. Opposite of out.
7. New Guinea (initials)
8. Aeroplanes do this.
11. Kingsford Smith's aeroplane was called 'Lady _____ Cross'
12. '_____' Claus.
13. P.G. Taylor was very _____ (courageous).
14. Sir Charles Kingsford Smith had this nickname.
19. P.G. Taylor's first name.
20. A honey-making insect.
21. George V was king of this country.
22. Road (abbreviation)
26. A person who flies aeroplanes.
28. All.
29. The Murray _____ forms the border between NSW and Victoria.
32. Opposite of short.
35. Favourite word of most cows.
37. Abbreviation for 'mister'

18. WHAT'S IN A NAME ?

What do *Santa Claus, Boring, Truth Or Consequences* and *Hell* all have in common? And what about Taumatawhakatangihangakoauatanenularangikitanatahu? The answer is that all are the names of places – very unusual names. The first three are in USA, while you must travel to Norway if you wish to visit Hell. The last place name is given to a hill in New Zealand. It translates to the *hill where the Great Husband of Heaven played his flute to his beloved*. Australia also has its share of unusual place names.

Many come from the local Aboriginal languages. Woy Woy, (NSW) means ' much water ', Wagga Wagga (NSW) means ' place of many crows' and Walla Walla (NSW), ' plenty of rain '. If a word coming from an Aboriginal language is repeated, as is the case with these names, there is a sense of many of a certain feature.

Ballarat (Victoria) from the local Aboriginal language means ' a resting place'. The local Aboriginal people often made camp at the lake that is now part of the city, Lake Wendouree.

Many Australian place names come directly from other countries. Captain Cook gave the East coast of Australia the name New South Wales. The countryside reminded him of Southern Wales. Newcastle and Swansea (both in NSW) are named after cities with the same names in England and Wales. Perth (WA) is named after Perth in Scotland.

At the time that Australia was being settled by Europeans there were numerous wars on the European continent. Some places are named after battlegrounds or battles. Waterloo (NSW) and Trafalgar (Victoria) are named after European battlegrounds. Camperdown (NSW and Victoria) was the name given to a famous sea battle in which Australia's fourth Governor, William Bligh, was involved. Balaklava (SA) is named after a famous battle during the Crimean War of 1854.

Some places were named after ships that were wrecked nearby. Collaroy, Malabar and Coolangatta (all in NSW) are named after shipwrecks.

Duplication was the reason for changing some place names. Australia had many places called Boat Harbour. The citizens of the Boat Harbour near Gosford in NSW decided that a change was necessary to avoid confusion. The boat was changed to its French equivalent, bateau. The new name became Bateau Bay. Another name change came about to one of the two places named Billabong in NSW. The Billabong near Cootamundra on the South West slopes of NSW had some letters removed at the front and back to give it the new name of Illabo.

The strangely named Tom Ugly's Point in Sydney is believed to have come from the mispronunciation by local Aborigines of the name of a well-known resident – Tom Huxley.

The barren Nullarbor Plain sounds like it could be an Aboriginal name but it is simply a combination of two Latin words. Null means 'no' and arbor means 'tree'.

The town of Holbrook near Albury (both in NSW) was named after Lieutenant Norman Holbrook. During World War 1 Lieutenant Holbrook had, daringly, taken his submarine up the narrow waters of the Dardanelles and sunk a number of Turkish warships. For his brave action he received the highest honour available to an Australian soldier, the Victoria Cross. Even if Lieutenant Holbrook had not done this, the township would still have been given a new name. Its name was Germantown and Germany was Australia's enemy during that war. The name of every town, street or locality has a story behind it. See if you can find out some of the stories in your district.

COMPREHENSION

A. Write short answers below.

1. Where can you go to visit Hell? _____

2. From which languages do the place names Woy Woy and Walla Walla come?

3. What does it mean if a name is repeated in some aboriginal languages?

   _____

4. Why did Captain James Cook name Australia's east coast **New South Wales**?

   _____

5. After what are Waterloo and Trafalgar named? _____

6. After what are **Collaroy**, **Malabar** and **Coolangatta** named? _____

7. What is the town near Gosford that was once named **Boat Harbour** now called?

   _____

8. Which NSW town was once called **Billabong**? _____

9. After whom is **Tom Ugly's Point** in Sydney named?

   _____

10. What do the Latin words **null** and **arbor** mean?
    NULL = _____ARBOR = _____

11. Which NSW town was once called
    Germantown?_____

12. **Perth** is named after a city in this country._____

B. Find words with these meanings in the text. Some letters are given.

1. the after effects of some actions __ __ __ __ e __ __ e __ __ __ __

2. many __ __ m __ __ o __ __

3. the act of pronouncing incorrectly __ __ __ __ __ r __ __ __ __ __ c __ __ __ __ o __

4. someone who lives at a certain place __ __ s __ d __ __ __

5. bravely __ __ __ __ __ g __ __

C. Write numerals inside the brackets in alphabetical order. Numbers 1, 2 and 3 are already done.

a. Woy Woy (_____)

b. Wagga Wagga (_____)

c. Walla Walla (_____)

d. Cardiff (_____)

e. Newcastle (_____)

f. Swansea (_____)

g. Perth (_____)

h. Camperdown (_____)

i. Cootamundra (_____)

j. Balaklava (____2_____)

k. Gosford (_____)

l. Illabo (_____)

m. Ballarat (____3_____)

n. Albury (____1____)

o. Holbrook (_____)

ACTIVITY

WHAT'S IN A NAME ENRICHMENT CAPITAL CITIES

The capital city names can be found in the puzzle. Words read letter to letter in any direction except diagonally. Every letter has been used. No letter is shared by words. One example is done. Colour answer blocks that connect each other different colours.

> **Buenos Aires Suva Stockholm London Tokyo Moscow**
> **Washington DC Brasilia Wellington Harare Jakarta Canberra Jerusalem**
> **Rome Paris Beijing Santiago Berlin New Delhi Cairo**

C	O	T	S	B	E	A	B	E	I	J	I
K	N	C	A	N	R	R	B	U	E	G	N
H	E	N	J	A	K	A	Y	K	N	O	N
O	W	O	M	O	S	R	O	O	A	S	O
L	D	D	W	O	C	T	A	T	I	R	T
M	E	N	C	A	I	R	O	S	S	E	G
J	L	O	A	R	O	M	E	I	R	A	N
E	H	L	I	L	I	P	A	R	E	R	I
R	I	B	R	A	S	S	U	V	A	A	L
U	M	S	O	G	A	R	L	I	N	H	L
S	E	A	N	T	I	E	B	C	D	N	E
A	L	W	A	S	H	I	N	G	T	O	W

Now match each capital city with its country.

1. The capital of the United Kingdom is_____.

2. _____ is Australia's capital.

3. Brazil's capital is _____

4. China's capital is _____

5. USA's capital is _____

6. _____ is Egypt's capital city.

7. New Zealand's capital is_____

8. Chile's capital is _____

9. India's capital is _____

10. Argentina's capital is _____

11. Germany's capital is _____

12. _____ is capital of Zimbabwe.

13. France's capital is _____

14. _____ is Fiji's capital.

15. _____ is capital of Indonesia.

16. Japan's capital is _____

17. Russia's capital is _____

18. Italy's capital is _____

19. Israel's capital is _____

20. _____ is Sweden's capital.

INDICATORS & OUTCOMES	a. answers literal questions
	b. uses context to find out the meanings of words
	c. is able to alphabetise

19. GALMAHRA (JACKEY-JACKEY) AND KENNEDY

Galmahra was an aborigine whose tribe came from the area around Muswellbrook, New South Wales. Being a good worker with a good knowledge of the bush he was chosen by the explorer, Edmund Kennedy, to join an expedition to Cape York Peninsula. Kennedy and his men called him by the name Jackey-Jackey.

The party set off in 1848. They wanted to find out if the area was suitable for farming. The first stage took them by ship to Rockingham Bay, near the present-day town of Tully.

Here Kennedy, Galmahra and eleven others disembarked from their ship, Tam O'Shanter. Their mission was to travel overland to Cape York to meet a ship called Ariel. From Ariel they would pick up more supplies and travel down the west coast of the peninsula.

The land from Rockingham Bay to the peninsula was thickly wooded with rainforests and mangroves. The expedition was poorly equipped to travel in such country. Their supplies were carried on two large, heavy carts. These bogged easily and were hard to manoeuvre in the rugged terrain. To complicate matters further they had brought along 100 sheep to see how they adapted to the country.

As the party progressed slowly over the rough country, supplies began to run low. They had to eat the sheep and some of the horses to survive.

Eventually the party reached a remote place called Weymouth Bay. Kennedy suggested that eight of the men make camp there and that he, Galmahra and three others continue on. Six of the eight men were to die at that camp. After a few days the three men accompanying Kennedy and Galmahra could not go on. They stopped to rest but were never seen again.

Kennedy became ill and Galmahra carried him for more than three kilometres. Finally they reached the Escape River and saw the Ariel in the distance on the other side. At the same time they came into contact with a fierce local tribe.

The tribesmen followed them for a day and a half before attacking them. Kennedy was speared and Galmahra had to shoot to keep the attackers away. Galmahra took Kennedy's notes and struggled on for ten days. To avoid the fierce local aborigines he often risked wading through deep crocodile-infested waters.

At last he reached the Ariel. When news of his loyalty and determination was heard in the colony he became regarded as a hero. He was given a grant of some money by the government.

Sadly, Galmahra developed a liking for alcohol. He died in 1854 when, affected by liquor, he fell face down into a camp fire and died of his burns. The people of the colony were saddened to learn that a man with such admirable qualities of friendship, loyalty and bravery had died so tragically.

GALMAHRA AND KENNEDY CROSSWORD

Across

2. A narrow strip of land that justs out into the sea.
8. _____ York
9. Western Australia (initials).
10. As well as.
11. Short for Alan.
12. Great Dividing Range (initials).
16. Royal Mail (initials).
18. Rugby Union (initials).
19. An animal used to pull the carts.
21. The ship that took Kennedy was supposed to meet when he reached Cape York.
27. Post Office (initials).
28. Rugby Union (initials)
29. Apart from Galmahra, only this number of men survived the journey.
31. Opposite to off.
32. south west (initials).
34. High School (initials)
36. Pigs love to lie in this.
37. Belonging to him.
39. You can record your voice on a cassette _____.
41. People live in one.
42. A tooth _____ is painful.
44. Short form of the word 'advertisement'.
46. Galmahra's tribe came from this area.
48. Money you get for working.
49. Finish.

Down

1. He was know as 'Jackey Jackey' by the white men, but his real name was _____ .
3. Something you can eat boiled, fried or scrambled.
4. north west (initials).
5. South Australia (initials).
6. Los Angeles (initials).
7. Small biting insects.
8. A dray is a type of _____.
13. A heavy cart.
14. To move quickly.
15. Ariel waited at Cape _____.
17. Capital city of Italy.
19. When people heard of what Galmahra had done he became a national _____.
20. Kennedy's first name.
22. Some people sprinkle this on their food.
23. Water comes out of one of these.
28. The country they went through was very _____.
30. You and I.
32. Ariel and Tam O'Shanter were there.
33. West Indies (initials).
34. I have, he ___.
35. Weapon used to kill Kennedy.
38. Kennedy took one hundred of these on the journey.
39. Town near Rockingham Bay.
40. They made a _____ at Weymouth Bay.
43. Something you eat on your birthday.
45. A spot.
47. French word that means 'the'.

20. 'MUM SHIRL' SMITH

Colleen Shirley Perry was born on an Aboriginal mission in NSW in 1924. She was one of fourteen children and quickly learnt the importance of sharing and giving. This is what she continued doing all of her adult life, helping those in need. Because she was a motherly figure to those she helped, she came to be known as 'Mum Shirl'.

Shirley's grandparents played an important part in her upbringing. Her grandfather, Budjarn, influenced her a great deal. He used to say to her, 'You have to first love yourself, and spread it around.' Colleen described him as 'the most powerful and gentlest man that God gave breath to.'

In the 1930s, when she was still quite young, her family moved to Sydney. It was here that one of her brothers got into trouble and was sent to gaol. Shirley visited him frequently and became a friend of other prisoners there. She saw that many of them had similar problems. Many felt isolated, unloved and without hope. This had led them to do things that were destructive to themselves and to others.

It was in the prisons that she got the nickname 'Mum Shirl'. If a prison authority asked her what her relationship with a particular prisoner was, she would say, 'I'm his Mum.'

Like the 'Mum' she was called, Shirley listened to them. Then she did what she could to help them.

Recognising the good work she was doing, prison authorities gave her access to many prisons in NSW. She would travel from one end of the state to another. For transport she relied on her family and friends. As well as helping those in gaol, she helped others in danger of losing hope by providing them with shelter. Her house was always full.

Mum Shirl could see that many of the Aboriginal people of her community in Redfern (a suburb of Sydney) were in poor health. In 1971 she played an important part in opening the first Aboriginal Medical Service. If she saw that someone needed medical attention but did nothing about it, she would practically drag them into the clinic, according to people who worked there.

Shirley died in 1998. There is a plaque outside Redfern's Saint Vincent's Church that honours her life. On it is the following tribute: In celebration of the life of Mum Shirl, the black saint of Redfern, who gave aid and comfort for all who asked.

Mum Shirl's special, selfless caring has influenced many lives for the better. Her life was devoted to her grandfather's philosophy of 'first love yourself and spread it around

COMPREHENSION

'MUM SHIRL' SMITH COMPREHENSION

A. Write short answers to the questions.

   1.   What was Mum Shirl's real name? _____

2. How many children were in her family? _____

3. What was her grandfather's name? _____

4. What special message did he give to Shirley? _____

5. To where did the family move in the 1930s? _____

6. What happened to one of Shirley's brothers? _____

7. What did she seem like to many of the prisoners? _____

8. What did she help establish in 1971? _____

B. Do you think you are wiser now than when you were in Kindergarten?
Do you expect to be wiser when you are 18 years old?
Do you expect to continue learning things through your experiences after you turn 18?
One of the cornerstones of Aboriginal culture is respect for elders.

In a few sentences why you think respect for elders is important.

_____

_____

_____

C. Find words with these meanings on the information page. The first letter is given.

1. often f __ __ __ __ __ __ __ __

2. alone i __ __ __ __ __ __ __

3. damaging d __ __ __ __ __ __ __ __ __ __

4. had an effect i __ __ __ __ __ __ __ __ __

D. Write the dictionary meaning of COMPASSION.

_____

_____

E. Make words of three letters or more using the letters in COMPASSION.
No people's names or plurals. Fifteen is a good score.

_____

_____

INDICATORS & OUTCOMES	**a.** answers literal questions
	b. expresses an opinion
	c. can use context to work out the meaning of words
	d. can use a dictionary to find word meanings
	e. can do simple word puzzles

Choose the correct words from the word bank to complete the story of Grace Bussell and Sam Isaacs.

memory   after   hours   shipwreck   horse   dangerous   waves   deed

In 1838 a young English girl named Grace Darling was praised for her courage when she helped rescue the survivors of a (1)_____off the coast of England. Some years later Australia had its own special, courageous Grace. Her name was Grace Bussell.

She lived on a farm on Western Australia's south–west coast. Her family were pioneers in the district. The town of Busselton is named (2) _____them. In 1876 when she was just sixteen years old, a heroic (3)_____had her being hailed as Australia's Grace Darling.

The winds on this part of Western Australia's coast can be very (4)_____, and wild seas have claimed many ships there in the past.

One windy morning as Grace was helping her mother make a Christmas pudding, Sam Isaacs came riding up to the farmhouse at a full gallop. Sam was an aboriginal stockman who worked on the Bussell's farm.

Breathlessly, he told Grace and her mother that a steamship was wrecked off Calgardup Beach. Grace quickly saddled her (5) _____ and, together with Sam, galloped down to the beach. Here they could both see the enormous waves pounding the helpless ship, the Georgette. Many people in the water were shouting for help. The captain had already launched the only lifeboat but it had capsized, drowning most of the occupants. Clinging to whatever they could, the few remaining people on board thought that it would be just a matter of time before the (6)_____ claimed them as well.

Grace and Sam rode their horses onto the beach and, without thinking of their own safety urged them into the boiling surf. They signalled the survivors to grab and hold onto the stirrups, reins and saddle leathers so their brave horses could swim them back to the beach.

For four exhausting (7)_____ they continued to charge into the pounding waves, rescuing more than fifty people. Only eight drowned. The survivors were brought to the homestead, where they were given dry clothes and something to eat.

The story of Grace and Sam made headlines. For her bravery Grace was awarded the first Royal Humane Society Of Australasia silver medal as well as a gold watch from the British Government. Sam was awarded a bronze medal from the British Government . The state government awarded Sam one hundred acres of farmland on the Margaret River. Here, he and his wife raised their six children. The rock that the Georgette struck is now known as Isaac's Rock in (8) _____of Sam.

Imagine you are a rescue worker. Write a report of a rescue situation you attended. Your report should emphasise the facts in the order they occurred. Try not to be speculative.

_____

_____

_____

_____

_____

_____

_____

_____

_____

_____

_____

_____

_____

_____

22. AUSTRALIAN SONGBIRDS

For a country with such a small population, Australia has a proud record in the arts (music, theatre, painting, sculpture and writing). Four women who won respect for Australia on the world's stages were the singers Dame Nellie Melba, Gladys Moncrieff, June Bronhill and Dame Joan Sutherland.

Dame Nellie Melba

Nellie Melba (1861–1931) was born Helen Porter Mitchell in Melbourne. She called herself Melba after her home city. In 1887 Melba went to Europe to perform in some of the great opera houses. Fifteen years later, and by now world famous, she returned to tour Australia. Melba's career lasted until 1928. Two dishes, Peach Melba and Melba Toast, were named after her. Nellie gave many 'farewell 'concerts around the world. From this came the saying to do a Melba. This means to announce one's departure, but then make numerous comebacks. Nellie was a great pioneer. She set an example for the talented singers who followed her. Australian artists realised that they could be the equal of any in the world.

Gladys Moncrieff (1892–1976) began her singing career in Townsville, Queensland. For over 35 years Our Glad, as she was known, entertained audiences in Australia, New Zealand, England and South Africa. She appeared in war zones to entertain the troops who were serving during World War II and the Korean War.

Broken Hill in the 1950s

June Gough (1929–2005) was born in Broken Hill, New South Wales. After appearing in a number of competitions, the people of Broken Hill began to realise that they had a great talent in their midst. They raised enough money to allow her to go to England to study. In gratitude she changed her surname to Bronhill, after the city. June went on to have an illustrious career as a singer and stage actor.

Dame Joan Sutherland's (1926–2010) career spanned over 40 years. She was recognised as one ot the 20th century's finest voices. In Italy they called her La Stupenda, which means The Wonderful One . She made more complete operatic recordings than any other singer in history. She frequently returned to Australia to give performances.

The music of great composers and performing artists enriches our lives.

COMPREHENSION

A. Write short answers to the questions below.

1. What was Nellie Melba's real name? _____

2. Why did she choose Melba as a stage name? _____

3. Where did she go to perform? _____

4. Which two dishes were named after her?_____
   _____ and _____ – _____

5. What does 'to do a Melba 'mean? _____

   _____

   _____

6. What did Australian performers begin to realise as a result of Melba's example?

_____

_____

7. Where did Gladys Moncrieff's singing career begin? _____

8. By what name was Gladys affectionately known? _____

9. What was June Bronhill's real name? _____

10. After which city did she take on her stage name? _____

11. What nickname was Joan Sutherland given? _____

12. What does this nickname mean? _____

B. Match the words to the songs. Write the song titles beside their words. (Hint: Type the words into a computer search engine.)

> **The Drover's Dream   On The Road To Gundagai   Waltzing Matilda**
> **Our Don Bradman   I've Been Everywhere   Advance Australia Fair**

1. 'There's a track winding back..."   _____

2. 'Who is it that all Australia raves about... '_____

3. 'Beneath our radiant Southern Cross... '_____

4. 'Under the shade of a coolabah tree...'_____

5. 'One day while travelling sheep, my companions lay asleep... '

_____

6. 'Crossed the deserts fair, Man...'   _____

C. A STATEMENT is a sentence that tells us something.

A QUESTION is a sentence that asks something.
The sentence below is mixed up. Use all the words to write a STATEMENT, then a QUESTION.

> **June   born   was   Broken   Gough   Hill   in**

STATEMENT: _____

QUESTION: _____

D. SKIMMING Locate these words in the text then write them in the order in which they appear on the information page.

> **enriches   farewell   example   population   gratitude   serving   pioneer**

_____

_____

23. AUSTRALIAN QUEENS OF THE TENNIS COURT

Have you ever picked up a tennis racquet and ball and just enjoyed the fun of hitting the ball against a wall? You can play all sorts of imaginary games doing this. You might play a cricket test. List your team and count the number of single bounce hits until the ball bounces more than once. When this happens the number of hits is counted as the batter's score and is written on your score sheet. A nice, flat wall would be useful for this game. Perhaps you have other similar games that you can play all by yourself. Many of Australia's great sportspeople began perfecting their skills playing such simple games.

Two Australian women who were recognised as ranking among the world's best players in their time were Margaret Court and Evonne Cawley. If you look in a book or on the internet you may see them listed with different surnames. Many of the tennis tournaments they won were before their marriages. Margaret's maiden name was Smith and Evonne's was Goolagong.

Margaret was born in Albury, on the New South Wales – Victorian border in 1942.

She won the Australian singles title eleven times between 1960 and 1973. This is a record that will probably never be beaten. She won the world's best known title, at Wimbledon in England (also called the British Open) three times. In 1979 she won the Grand Slam (the French, British, Australian and US titles in one year). On three other occasions (1962, 1969 and 1973) she missed out on the Grand Slam by losing only one of these four titles. Margaret married the son of Western Australian Premier and himself, later, Premier of Western Australia, Sir Charles Court.

Evonne Cawley grew up in the NSW country town of Barellan. As a child she used to practise her tennis strokes hitting a ball against a wooden fence for hours.

This young Aboriginal girl surprised and delighted the world when, at the age of nineteen, she won the 1971 Wimbledon women's title. She went on to win many other titles.

Hume Dam near Albury

Evonne's daughter, Kelly, was born in 1977. When Evonne won Wimbledon for the second time in 1980, she was the first mother to win this title since Dorothy Chalmers in 1914. Evonne was always the favourite of tennis crowds because of her gracious behaviour. Both Evonne and Margaret are regarded as tennis legends, not only in Australia but worldwide.

ACTIVITY

A. Write short answers to the questions below.

1. What was Margaret's maiden name? _____

2. What was Evonne's maiden name? _____

3. When and where was Margaret born? _____

4. How many times did Margaret win the Australian singles title?

_____

5. By what other name is the Wimbledon championship known?

_____

6. Which titles must a player win in one year to have won a Grand Slam?

_____

7. In which NSW town did Evonne grow up? _____

8. How did Evonne practise when she was a young girl?

_____

9. How old was Evonne when she won her first Wimbledon title?

_____

10. What is the name of Evonne's daughter? _____

11. Who was the previous mother to win Wimbledon? _____

12. In which year did Dorothy win this Wimbledon title? _____

B. Use the tennis terms in the word bank to complete the sentences.

Davis Cup doubles umpire receiver strings love server lob

1. Zero in tennis is called _____.

2. The person hitting the ball first in a point of tennis is called the

_____.

3. The person who hits the ball second in a point of tennis is called
the_____.

4. The person in charge of the game is called the _____.

5. A ball hit high in the air is called a _____.

6. When two people play as a team against two others it is known as

_____.

7. Countries play against each other for a trophy known as the_____

_____.

8. You hit the ball on the racquet's _____.

C. See how many words of three letters or more you can make using the letters in
TENNIS BALL. No PROPER NOUNS or PLURALS. Twenty is a good score.

_____

_____

D. Make up the rules for your own special game. List the equipment you need as well
as the rules. Keep it simple. No more than five rules.

_____

_____

24. AUSTRALIAN INVENTORS

Australia's distance from other countries has advantages and disadvantages. One by-product of our isolation is that Australians have had to become very self-reliant.

The aerodynamic properties of the boomerang are the basis of the screw propeller on boats and ships. T L Mitchell first drew attention to this in 1850.

The main aim of early European settlers was to be successful farmers in the new land. John Ridley came to Australia with his family in 1839. He was a miller. The summer of 1842–3 produced an excellent wheat harvest. There was, however, a shortage of workers to reap it. The South Australian government offered a reward to anyone who could devise a machine that would harvest these crops. Ridley invented his stripper which harvested and threshed the wheat in one action. Ridley could have become rich if he had patented his invention, but he saw it as his gift to the colony that had made him prosperous.

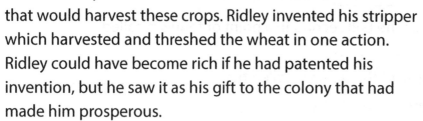

Maria Ann Smith gave the world the first 'Granny Smith 'apples from her Sydney farm. The discovery was something of an accident, as one tree grew from some Tasmanian apple seeds that she had planted in a paddock.

In 1876 Robert Bowyer Smith invented a plough that could be used in country where tree stumps had not been cleared. He named it the 'stump jump 'plough.

Hugh Victor McKay improved on Ridley's stripper. His 'Sunshine Harvester ' cut wheat, threshed it (removed the useful part) and cleaned it ready for milling.

By 1912 there were tensions in Europe that were to lead to World War I. L E de Mole invented an armoured vehicle which moved by means of a continuous tracked belt. This was the world's first army tank. (World War I plunged the world into conflict from 1914 to 1918.)

Aspirin was a German patented medicine. Because Australia was at war with Germany supplies of this medication were withheld. George Nicholas and H W Smith, two chemists, discovered how it could be produced. They sold it under the trade name 'Aspro'.

1923 was a landmark year for two Australian favourites. In that year Doctor C P Callister invented the vegetable extract which he called 'Vegemite'. In the same year Hoadley's Chocolate company developed the Violet Crumble Bar.

Lewis Brandt worked for the Ford Motor Company in Geelong, Victoria. In 1934 he came up with an idea for a vehicle that would be useful for farm work. His bosses liked it and soon began manufacturing these vehicles which they called utilities.

RG Whitehead wanted to make a powerful glue for everyday household repairs. By 1935 he had succeeded and sold his invention under the name of 'Tarzan's Grip'.

Sunshine Bakeries of Newtown, Sydney, came up with a novel idea in 1939. It was then that they sold the first sliced bread.

In 1946 Lance Hill produced a rotary clothes line that was to become a feature of many Australian backyards. He named it the 'Hill's Hoist'.

F G McEnroe of Bendigo also pleased Australian taste buds with his 1951 invention of the 'Chiko Roll'.

Mervyn Victor Richardson's 1952 invention of a lawnmower which used rotating blades delighted gardeners. He sold it as the 'Victa 'lawnmower.

In 1961 the Malleys company invented a lightweight insulated food container designed to keep food and drinks cool. It was sold under the trade name 'Esky'.

Who knows what the next useful invention will be!

A. Rule lines to match the person with their invention or discovery. Use a number of different colours.

Hugh Victor McKay	army tank
Lance Hill	stripper – harvester
Mervyn Victor Richardson	Granny Smith apples
Lewis Brandt	sliced bread
John Ridley	stump – jump plough
Sunshine Bakeries	Chiko Roll
Maria Ann Smith	Hills Hoist
F G McEnroe	Victa lawnmower
L E de Mole	Sunshine Harvester
Robert Bowyer Smith	utility car

B. Use the code to complete the sentences about Australian inventions.

**Code: A=! B=@ C=# D=$ E=% F=^ G=& H=* I=(J=) K=+ L={ M=} N=< O=>
P=? Q=- R=/ S=\ T=| U= = V=... W=$% X=" Y=<> Z=;**

A. The surf lifesaving reel was first demonstrated in 1906 by its inventor, ____ ____

____ ____ ____ ____ Ormsby.   { <> \ | % /

B. Louis ____ ____ ____ ____ ____ ____ ____ invented the torpedo in 1877. . @ / %

< < ! <

C. The ____ ____ __ ____ ____ ____ ____ was first made by Herbert Sachse of

Perth's Esplanade Hotel. . ? ! ... { > ... !

D. Howard ____ ____ ____ ____ ____ ____ helped develop the wonder drug,

penicillin.   . ^ { > / % <>

E. Depending on how it affects you, change brings with it advantages and disadvantages. The motor car was great news for many people but terrible news for blacksmiths and horse dealers. Answer the questions below in sentences.

1. How have automatic teller machines improved life?

_____

_____

2. What are some disadvantages of automatic teller machines?

_____

_____

F. List two inventions you'd like to see made. Example: bed making machine

1.

_____

_____

2.

_____

_____

25. SAME MESSAGE, DIFFERENT METHODS

Travelling from England to Australia with the First Fleet in 1788 was the colony's first chaplain, the Reverend Richard Johnson. He was a kindly man who always tried to see the best in people. To many of the new settlers his kindness and gentle manners were seen as weakness. Church attendances began to decline. Little encouragement to attend church was given by the Governor or his officers. They seldom attended themselves.

When Governor Hunter replaced Captain Phillip he ordered that convicts should attend Sunday church services. He saw this as being a useful way of controlling the convicts. This did not prove to be the case, however, as many convicts resented the order. In 1798 a convict set alight the small

Governor Phillip

church which the Reverend Johnson had built, largely with his own money. Thereafter until a new church was eventually built, church services were held in a sandstone storehouse. To ensure that the convicts did not benefit from the action of the arsonist, Governor Hunter made a new decree that convicts attend church twice on Sundays.

Many people blamed the Reverend Johnson for Governor Hunter's action. This put the shy, sensitive clergyman in an awkward position. The hard work of earlier years and these new stresses had an effect on his health. He returned to England in 1800 where he remained until his death in 1827.

The Reverend Samuel Marsden , one of the Reverend Johnson's assistants, took charge of the colony's religious functions in 1800.

While the Reverend Marsden generally followed Christian principles he was far more forceful than his predecessor in doing this.

The convicts soon saw that Marsden would be a lot more difficult to deal with than the Reverend Johnson had been. Various schemes were devised to get rid of him. On one occasion a convict standing near Marsden, and by the waterside, appeared to trip and fall into the water.

Even though this man was a very good swimmer he made motions as if he was drowning.

Being a true Christian who was dedicated to saving his fellow man, Marsden dived into the water with the intention of saving what he took to be a drowning man. As soon as the clutching man took hold of Marsden he tried to drown his would-be rescuer.

Marsden overpowered him, dragged the convict ashore and flogged him soundly for his ill-fated misdeed.

Rev. Samuel Marsden.

As well as attending to religious matters, Marsden was also a magistrate. He was severe in handing out punishment to those he judged to have broken the law. He found that his two jobs, one as a magistrate and the other as a preacher , allowed him to mete out his own special mixed brand of justice.

When a man complained that he could not get his wife to do housework Marsden visited the home and punished the woman by flogging her with a horsewhip. It is easy to see why he was given the name the Flogging Parson.

Marsden successfully carried out some missionary work in New Zealand. The native Maori people and the European settlers and whalers were constantly at war with each other. They would attempt to kill each other on sight. Marsden thought that his missionaries, if allowed to preach the Christian message, could make a difference and bring about a peaceful solution to the problem.

Marsden, with only one assistant, visited one of the most feared Maori leaders. He explained that the missionaries aim was to bring about peace, not to rob and plunder. To prove his good intentions he slept one night by the side of the Maori leader.

The Maoris were impressed by his courage in doing this and they allowed his preachers to go about their work unhindered.

Samuel Marsden was 73 when he died in 1838. While many people mourned his passing, so too did many silently rejoice.

SAME MESSAGE, DIFFERENT METHODS COMPREHENSION

A. Write short answers below.

1. Who was the first chaplain in Australia?

_____

2. What sort of man was he?

_____

3. What did some people think his kindness was a sign of?

_____

4. How could the officers have helped boost church attendances?

_____

5. Who replaced Captain Phillip as Governor?

_____

6. Why did this new governor think church attendance was a good thing?

_____

7. What happened to the colony's little church in 1798?

_____

8. How did Governor Hunter punish the convicts for burning down the church?

_____

9. Where were church services held until a new church was built?

_____

10. When did the Reverend Johnson return to England?

_____

11. Who took charge of religious matters when Reverend Johnson left Australia?

_____

12. How did the convicts feel about Marsden?

_____

13. What did Marsden do to the convict who tried to drown him?

_____

14. What nickname was Marsden given?

_____

15. How did the Maoris feel about Marsden?

_____

B. As far as we know, the people on the First Fleet were Christians. Name three of the world's other main religions.

_____

_____

C. Write dictionary definitions to answer the following.

1. What is an ATHEIST?

_____

_____

2. What is an AGNOSTIC?

_____

_____

D. Find words in the text that match the meanings. Some letters are given.

1. not often __ __ __ d __ __

2. after this __ __ __ __ __ __ f __ __ r

3. a judge __ __ __ __ s t __ __ __ __

4. native of New Zealand __ __ __ __ __ __

INDICATORS & OUTCOMES	**a.** answers literal questions
	b. and
	c. uses the internet as a research tool
	d. can use context to work out the meaning of words

26. FANNY DURACK AUSTRALIAN WOMEN'S SWIMMING PIONEER

When Fanny Durack was born in Sydney in 1891 public swimming by women was regarded as 'unladylike'. As one critic put it, women's swimming 'coarsened females who indulged in it both physically and morally'. In spite of this many women risked becoming outcasts – enough to warrant some of the few public baths in Sydney at the time to have a 'Ladies' Hour'.

Fanny taught herself to swim at Coogee Baths. By the age of nine she was a proficient swimmer. When she was a teenager she developed her own style which was based on a stroke used by Native Americans. This stroke was known as the *trudgen stroke*. It allowed the swimmer to swim faster than other strokes used by competitors in *freestyle* races. In a *freestyle* race any stroke may be used to complete the course. The stroke favoured by most swimmers nowadays is the *Australian Crawl* also known as the *front crawl*.

Fanny had read about and seen pictures of Australia's first great woman swimmer, Annette Kellerman. She decided that she wanted to be like Annette Kellerman.

At that time, however, there were no competitive swimming events for women and very few for girls.

When she entered an event for girls at Sydney's Cleveland Street Baths she was soundly defeated. This affected her enthusiasm and she did not enter another girls' race for two years. Her return to competition was in a thirty-three yard (thirty metre) event which was included in a boys' carnival at Lavender Bay. Arriving late at the carnival she climbed the closed gate and barely made it to the starting board in time. Fanny was defeated by Mina Wylie, a girl who was to be her great rival.

Fanny continued competitive swimming and won many titles. She had been using her version of the trudgen stroke in freestyle races but had studied a new stroke known as the *Australian Crawl*. This had become the stroke favoured by the leading male swimmers of the time, Alec Wickham and Cecil Healey. When she used this stroke for the first time in a 100 metre race she slashed six seconds from her previous best time.

In 1912 the Olympic Swimming Selection Committee was choosing the swimming team for the Stockholm Olympics. There was opposition to including women on the Australian team.

It had never happened before. Because there was only one swimming event for women at these games some suggested it was not worth the cost of sending a woman swimmer to the games. A public fund was opened by Mrs Hugh D McIntosh, a swimming official. The huge public support for this caused the selection committee to back down and Fanny and her great rival, Mina Wylie were chosen to compete. This was a great breakthrough for Australian women's sport.

The two young women did not let their supporters down. Fanny won the only women's race, the 100 metres, by four body lengths. Mina finished second of the five competitors after being last on turning for the last lap of the pool.

Fanny had become the first Australian woman to win an Olympic gold medal. She had inspired other girls to take up the sport.

Fanny continued to train and compete in the hope of defending her Olympic title at the 1916 games. Sadly, the terrible conflict, World War One, intervened and the games did not go ahead. She was chosen to compete in the 1920 games but suffered an attack of appendicitis a week before the team departed and stayed at home.

After this disappointment Fanny decided to retire from competition and concentrate on coaching.

At the opening of the Wagga Olympic Pool in 1954 Fanny was officially the first person to enter the water. She gave a demonstration swim over 100 metres, the distance she swam to win Olympic gold forty-two years earlier. A year after opening the Wagga Olympic Pool Fanny died.

Her name, however, continues to be held in high regard. Sydney's Petersham Park Swimming Park was renamed Fanny Durack Aquatic Centre in 1999.

A. Write short answers below.

1. When and where was Fanny Durack born?

_____

2. How was public swimming by women regarded at this time?

_____

3. What did some swimming baths do to cater for female swimmers?

_____

4. What is meant by a 'Ladies'Hour'?

_____

5. Who taught Fanny to swim?

_____

6. Where did she learn to swim?

_____

7. What is the name of the swimming stroke that was developed by Native Americans?

_____

8. What stroke does a swimmer use in a freestyle race?

_____

9. Which stroke do most swimmers use when swimming in a freestyle race (2 names)?

_____

10. Who was Australia's first great woman swimmer?

_____

11. At which Sydney baths did she enter her first swimming race for women?

_____

12. What was the distance of her return race two years after her first race?

_____

13. Who defeated Fanny in this race?

_____

14. Which two male swimmers were having great success using the Australian Crawl stroke?

_____

15. How many seconds did Fanny cut from her best 100 metres time using the Australian Crawl stroke?

_____

16. In which city were the 1912 Olympics held?

_____

17. How many women's swimming races were held at these games?

_____

18. Who opened a public fund to pay for Fanny and Mina Wylie's travel to Stockholm?

_____

19. What was Fanny the first Australian woman to do?

_____

20. Why were the 1916 Olympics cancelled?

_____

21. What stopped Fanny from competing in the 1920 Olympics?

_____

22. At the opening of which public pool did Fanny swim in 1954?

_____

B. A **cliché** (pronounced klee-shay) is an expression that has lost much of its meaning because of overuse. Example: Bruce will **have an uphill battle** defeating Jack in their upcoming tennis match. It is not considered good practice to use **clichés** in writing or commentary (but at times, it is hard not to).

Highlight or underline the sporting clichés below.

1. The coach said Bailey was the best thing since sliced bread. He was on fire today! (two clichés)

2. Neither team won tonight. Rugby League was the winner.

3. You could hear a pin drop as Bloggs lined up his putt.

4. The Swans gave 110 percent today.

5. Young Jake Wardman played like a man possessed.

INDICATORS & OUTCOMES	**a.** answers literal questions
	b. identifies clichés in a text

Use the code to spell the words. Put the words in the blanks on the information sheet.

1.
$\overline{}$ $\overline{}$ $\overline{}$ $\overline{}$
5 + 9 18 + 2 22 + 10 42 − 10

2.
$\overline{}$ $\overline{}$ $\overline{}$ $\overline{}$ $\overline{}$
11 + 9 12 x 1 40 + 8 40 − 8 30 + 40

3.
$\overline{}$ $\overline{}$ $\overline{}$ $\overline{}$
15 + 15 10 x 4 7 x 2 5 x 10

4.
$\overline{}$ $\overline{}$ $\overline{}$ $\overline{}$ $\overline{}$
8 x 5 2 x 11 34 + 20 9 + 11 30 + 8

5.
$\overline{}$ $\overline{}$ $\overline{}$ $\overline{}$ $\overline{}$ $\overline{}$ $\overline{}$
2 x 8 29 + 3 1 x 12 7 x 4 4 x 9 8 + 12 9 x 2

6.
$\overline{}$ $\overline{}$ $\overline{}$ $\overline{}$ $\overline{}$ $\overline{}$ $\overline{}$
4 x 4 7 + 13 33 + 5 60 − 6 38 + 10 2 x 6 28 + 4

7.
$\overline{}$ $\overline{}$ $\overline{}$ $\overline{}$ $\overline{}$ $\overline{}$ $\overline{}$
27 + 5 6 + 14 6 x 2 2 x 9 8 + 20 34 + 4 8 x 3

8.
$\overline{}$ $\overline{}$ $\overline{}$ $\overline{}$ $\overline{}$ $\overline{}$ $\overline{}$ $\overline{}$
60 − 4 3 x 4 35 + 3 30 − 2 10 x 5 16 + 10 5 + 15 6 x 3

9.
$\overline{}$ $\overline{}$ $\overline{}$ $\overline{}$ $\overline{}$
9 x 6 50 − 2 8 + 4 8 x 2 4 x 5

10.
$\overline{}$ $\overline{}$ $\overline{}$ $\overline{}$
2 x 7 4 x 10 10 + 8 7 x 10

11.
$\overline{}$ $\overline{}$ $\overline{}$ $\overline{}$ $\overline{}$ $\overline{}$
3 x 6 5 x 4 30 + 20 13 + 7 4 x 12 6 x 9

12.
$\overline{}$ $\overline{}$ $\overline{}$ $\overline{}$ $\overline{}$ $\overline{}$
7 x 2 5 x 11 12 x 4 4 x 7 12 + 8 20 − 2

13.
$\overline{}$ $\overline{}$ $\overline{}$ $\overline{}$ $\overline{}$ $\overline{}$ $\overline{}$ $\overline{}$ $\overline{}$
7 x 6 30 − 10 50 + 4 14 + 6 8 x 6 9 x 4 7 + 5 28 + 10 40 − 2

14.
$\overline{}$ $\overline{}$ $\overline{}$ $\overline{}$ $\overline{}$
5 + 7 8 x 7 4 + 8 18 + 10 4 x 8

15.
$\overline{}$ $\overline{}$ $\overline{}$ $\overline{}$ $\overline{}$ $\overline{}$ $\overline{}$
8 + 6 15 + 5 8 x 4 20 + 8 16 + 4 7 x 8 17 + 3

16.
$\overline{}$ $\overline{}$ $\overline{}$ $\overline{}$ $\overline{}$ $\overline{}$
6 x 8 2 x 10 4 x 3 28 + 4 20 + 12 10 x 7

17.
$\overline{}$ $\overline{}$ $\overline{}$ $\overline{}$ $\overline{}$
10 x 2 56 + 5 7 x 4 20 + 30 44 + 10

A = 12 B = 14 C = 16 D = 18 E = 20 F = 22 G = 24 H = 26 I = 28 J = 30 K = 31 L = 32
M = 36 N = 38 O = 40 P = 42 Q = 44 R = 48 S = 50 T = 54 U = 55 V = 56 W = 60 X = 61
Y = 70 Z = 75

THINK ABOUT IT

No-one really knows if Lasseter found a reef. Some say it is a hoax. Why might he make up such a story?

COMPREHENSION

LASSETER'S LOST GOLD REEF – FACT OR FICTION ?

From the very earliest times gold has enchanted humankind. People have endured the worst of conditions to look for it. Terrible things have been done to acquire it. To some people it has been a craving which has cost them dearly.

Harold (1) __ __ __ __ Lasseter was someone who loved this precious metal. His search for gold and his disappearance are at the centre of one of Australia's great mysteries.

Lasseter was born in Victoria in 1880. Little is known of his (2) __ __ __ __ __ life but it seems that he was a man who changed (3) __ __ __ __ (4) __ __ __ __ __ . He spent several years in America and some time working on the Sydney Harbour Bridge.

In 1929 he told some people a story of a fabulous gold reef he (5) __ __ __ __ __ __ __ he had found in (6) __ __ __ __ __ __ __ Australia years earlier, in 1911. He said that it was about ten kilometres long and over three metres wide. This would have made it the world's richest reef.

He set off (7) __ __ __ __ __ __ __ an expedition in 1930 but it was unsuccessful. In 1931 he tried again. This time he (8) __ __ __ __ __ __ __ __ without a (9) __ __ __ __ __ .

A (10) __ __ __ __ was found in the (11) __ __ __ __ __ and was (12) __ __ __ __ __ __ in the (13) __ __ __ __ __ __ __ __ __ Ranges but is not clear that it was Lasseter's.

Several attempts were made to find the reef after this but to no (14) __ __ __ __ __ . Many people (15) __ __ __ __ __ __ __ that the reef doesn't (16) __ __ __ __ __ __ (17) __ __ __ __ __ but was a figment of Lasseter's imagination.

28. CRICKET – AUSTRALIA'S NATIONAL GAME

There's a breathless hush in the Close to-night—
Ten to make and the match to win—
A bumping pitch and a blinding light,
An hour to play and the last man in.
And it's not for the sake of a ribboned coat,
Or the selfish hope of a season's fame,
But his captain's hand on his shoulder smote
"Play up! play up! and play the game!"

So reads the first verse of the poem *Vitai Lampada* (meaning *the torch of life*) written in 1892 by the English poet, Henry Newbolt.

In the second verse we learn that the young man remembering the heroics on the cricket pitch is now a soldier. The special brand of courage and resourcefulness he learnt on the playing fields were the same as those he would call upon to save his friends and comrades in the battle that lay ahead.

Cricket is played in most countries that were colonised by England. It continues to play an important role in Australia's sporting fabric. Because it is played in all the states and territories, many think of it as our national game.

No doubt, cricket matches took place in the very early days of European settlement of Australia. The first recorded match for which scores were kept took place in 1826.

The game was loved not only as a sport. Many people followed it because they liked to gamble on the outcome.

An article appearing in the newspaper, *the Sydney Gazette* of 2 January 1830, refers to a match being played with over one hundred spectators watching. The report mentions the game being played 'for heavy stakes'.

Inter colonial matches began in 1851 when a team from Victoria travelled to Launceston to play a Tasmanian side. The Tasmanians won that match but the Victorians got their revenge the following year in a game played in Melbourne. The conditions were laid out in a Melbourne newspaper that was published just prior to play commencing:
"It is agreed that the wicket should be pitched at half – past eight (so) that the game might commence punctually at nine o'clock. At one o'clock the bugle will sound, when an adjournment from the field to the tents for half an hour will take place. " A few years later a team from Melbourne challenged a New South Wales team for a stake of £500 ($1 000), a very large sum at that time. The game was eventually played in Melbourne in March of 1856. The visitors won a stirring game with the scores being Victoria 63 and 28 and, New South Wales, 76 and 7 for 16. This match set up a rivalry between these two states that exists to this day.

A visiting *All England* eleven helped to further popularise the game when it came to Australia to play an exhibition match against a Victorian eighteen. Of this match one Melbourne journalist proudly reported: *"Of all the interesting games the MCG has witnessed, none has been so memorable as that on New Year's Day of 1862, when the first friendly rivalry in sports took place between the mother country and her growing daughters. What crowds of faces peered one*

behind another in that vast ring, looking forth on the men whose names were famous in connection with the national game! The greatest enthusiasm prevailed and, though the local team was defeated, the Melbourne people were proud that their champions had made so respectable a stand against the leading cricketers of the world."

In 1868 a team of Australian aboriginal cricketers made up Australia's first touring team to England. They acquitted themselves admirably winning 14 and losing 14 of 47 games with 19 being drawn.

The first ever Test Match was played in Melbourne in 1877. Australia won the game by 45 runs. Remarkably, the *Centenary Test* of 1977 was, again, won by Australia with a margin of 45 runs. The friendly rivalry continues to this day with test matches being played for a trophy called *the Ashes.*

The sound of a willow bat on a leather ball is familiar to most Australians. Like the young soldier in Henry Newbolt's poem, young men are learning important lessons testing themselves on the cricket pitches of Australia every summer.

COMPREHENSION

Write short answers below.

1. Which game is being referred to at the beginning of the article?

_____

2. How many runs were needed by the batting team to win the game?

_____

3. What words of encouragement did the captain give to his team mate?

_____

4. What does the title mean in English?

_____

5. Who wrote the poem?

_____

6. When was the poem written?

_____

7. What did the young man in the poem become when he grew up?

_____

8. Why do many people say that cricket is Australia's national game?

9. In which year were scores first recorded in an Australian cricket match?

10. Why else, apart from love of the game, was cricket popular in the early days of Australia's European colonisation?

11. Which early newspaper reported on a match played on 2 January 1830?

12. When was the first inter colonial match played?

13. Which two colonies played against each other in this game?

14. Where was this game played?

15. Who won this game?

16. What was sounded to signal a thirty minute break in this game?

17. What stake did New South Wales and Victoria play for in their 1856 game?

18. Which colony's team won this game?

19. How many players were in the Victorian team that played an All England eleven?

20. Who won this game?

21. What is meant by the Mother Country?

22. In which year did an aboriginal team tour England?

23. What was their win / loss / draw record in the 47 games they played?

W_____ L_____ D_____

24. When was the first test match played?

_____

ACTIVITY – ENRICHMENT

A. Cricket bats are made from the wood of the willow tree.

These trees love water. They are often seen growing on river banks. Their roots play an important role in holding the soil of the river bank together. This lessens erosion of river bank soil.

Over-clearing of trees can cause disastrous consequences. In 2006 in the province of Leyte in the Philippines, a mudslide covered the school at Guinsaugon village. Over 200 students and teachers lost their lives. This tragedy occurred after ten days of rain. Intensive tree logging had reduced tree numbers. This soaking and the absence of tree roots to bind the soil were blamed for the tragedy.

The tree names below are jumbled. Put them in the correct order.

Three letters:

a. m u g ___ ___ ___

b. h a s ___ ___ ___

c. k a o ___ ___ ___

d. r i f ___ ___ ___

e. w e y ___ ___ ___

f. m e l ___ ___ ___

Four letters:

a. k a t e ___ ___ ___ ___

b. l a m p ___ ___ ___ ___

c. l u m p ___ ___ ___ ___

d. p a r e ___ ___ ___ ___

e. t a d e ___ ___ ___ ___

f. n i p e ___ ___ ___ ___

B. Which tree appears on the flag of Lebanon?

_____

_____

C. The leaf of which tree appears on the flag of Canada?

_____

_____

D. Listed below in jumbled form are five ways a batter can be dismissed. Write them with the letters in correct order:

a. a g c u t h ___ ___ ___ ___ ___ ___

b. o w l b e d ___ ___ ___ ___ ___ ___

c. t e d s u m p ___ ___ ___ ___ ___ ___ ___

d. u r n u t o ___ ___ ___ ___ ___ ___

e. g e l r e b o f e t w i c k e ___ ___ ___ ___ ___ ___ ___ ___ ___ ___ ___ ___ ___ ___

E. What is 'the baggy green'?

_____

_____

F. What is the job of the umpire in a game of cricket?

_____

_____

G. What are the bails in cricket?

_____

_____

H. If you 'hit a boundary' in a cricket match, what do you do?

_____

_____

I. The fielding team must appeal to the umpire if they think a batter is out. What do they usually call out when appealing?

_____

_____

ANSWERS

1. GRANNY SMITH – COMPREHENSION

A.
1. England
2. Ryde (Sydney)
3. chickens, cows, apples
4. she sold them at market and they proved to be popular

B. A Wonder Of Nature – The Granny Smith Apple

C.
1. Maria, Ann
2. England, Australia

D.
1. orchard
2. unusual
3. husband
4. popular

E. teacher

Procedure – How To Make An Apple Pie teacher

2. LIFESAVERS COMPREHENSION

A. hot beach dangerous lifesavers safe

B.
1. William Gocher
2. 1902
3. New South Wales Surf Bathing Association

C.
1. safest
2. decided
3. followed
4. speak
5. trouble

D. NOUNS: summertime people beach swimming * surf (Note that swimming* here is a GERUND or VERBAL NOUN)
VERBS: visit, can be

E. teacher

LIFESAVERS ACTIVITY – SURFING

1. gremlin
2. catch
3. curl
4. Kahuna
5. breaker
6. wipeout
7. huarache
8. hang
9. baggies
10. grommet
11. woodie
12. Surf's up!
13. soup
14. tube
15. bombora
16. goofy
17. walking
18. ankle busters
19. ding
20. toes

PUZZLE ANSWERS: Mark Richards, Surfaris

3. CRAIG JOHNSTON – COMPREHENSION

A.
1. Booragul
2. Middlesborough
3. Liverpool
4. to help his family look after his sick sister

B. teacher

C.
1. exceptional
2. gamble
3. eventually

D. teacher

E. teacher

CRAIG JOHNSTON ACTIVITY SOCCER (FOOTBALL)

1. sweeper
2. stopper
3. penalty
4. gloves
5. yellow
6. red
7. shy
8. goalkeepers
9. Rimet
10. spherical
11. spectator
12. Socceroos
13. eleven
14. whistle
15. pass
16. corner
17. dribbling
18. pea
19. rules
20. referee
21. four
22. striker

PUZZLE MYSTERY TEAM = Wolverhampton Wanderers

4. CAROLINE CHISHOLM – COMPREHENSION

A.
1. India
2. 1838
3. employment (a job)
4. a shelter for unemployed girls
5. country areas
6. crowded
7. Sydney
8. 1846

B.
1. carol
2. car
3. line
4. his

C.
1. distressed
2. help
3. immigrants
4. individual
5. opportunities
6. unemployed

D. teacher

CAROLINE CHISHOLM – ACTIVITY

1. Abakerazum
2. George
3. Aba Mina
4. Andrew
5. Denis
6. Kilda
7. Vincent

Riddle 1: a riddle

8. Nicholas
9. Mary
10. Christopher
11. patron
12. Jude

Riddle 2: a road

13. Bernadette
14. canonization
15. Ruis
16. Gerard
17. Elizabeth
18. Patrick
19. James
20. Francis

Riddle 3: daughter Picture = a Saint Bernard

5. RESCUE WORKERS – PAUL FEATHERSTONE COMPREHENSION

A.
1. tourism, skiing
2. a landslide
3. the danger of being buried alive by further slides
4. ambulance paramedic
5. Stuart Diver

B. Winter time. Thredbo is a skiing resort and winter is the time when there is most snow.

C. Our Caring Rescue Workers

D.
1. bravery
2. danger
3. paramedic
4. dedication

E. teacher

RESCUE WORKERS PAUL FEATHERSTONE ENRICHMENT

A.
1. Kosciuszko
2. Bogong
3. Bimeri
4. Bartle Frere
5. Ossa
6. Zeil
7. Woodroffe
8. Meharry

B. McLintock, Nepal, Himalayas, Sagarmatha, Chomolungma

C. teacher

6. JOHN FLYNN – COMPREHENSION

A.
1. on the coastline
2. Minister of the Presbyterian Church
3. camel
4. fell from his horse
5. pedal radio transmitters

B. teacher

C.
1. remote
2. region
3. tragedies
4. homesteads
5. patient
6. boulder

D. He Worked To Help Others

E. information report

F. teacher

JOHN FLYNN – ACTIVITY HEALTH AND MEDICAL TERMS

1. dentist
2. pathologist
3. neurologist
4. chiropodist
5. antibiotics
6. optometrist
7. osteopath
8. respiratory
9. cardiology
10. paediatrician
11. audiologist
12. psychiatrist
13. dietician
14. acupuncture
15. orthodontist
16. dermatologist
17. herbalist
18. anaesthetist

PUZZLE: The Hippocratic Oath

7. OUR FLAG – COMPREHENSION

A. the states joined together to form the Commonwealth Of Australia

B.
1. 1 January 1901
2. The Review Of Reviews Of Australasia
3. £ 50 ($100)
4. a tobacco company
5. 32 823
6. the six states
7. the six states
8. the territories

C.
1. False (The Crimean War took place in 1854, many years before Australia had a national flag.)
2. False (There was a large number of entries.)

OUR FLAG VOCABULARY – ACTIVITY

1. estoile
2. vexillology
3. Glory
4. field
5. union
6. canton
7. ensign

PUZZLE: silence

8. staff
9. pall
10. vexillologist
11. fesses
12. hoist
13. halyard
14. charge
15. June
16. saltire

17. Star
18. finial
19. half-mast
20. pales

PUZZLE: a postage stamp

8. THE DAYS OF THE HAWKERS – COMPREHENSION

A.
1. a computer
2. groceries
3. hawkers
4. drummers
5. the feet / walking

B.
1. chinwag = a friendly chat to pass a bit of time
2. Wilcannia Shower = a dust storm
3. Shank's pony = the legs
4. a cuppa = a social cup of tea
5. a run = the route travelled by a hawker to sell goods
6. a Southerly buster = a strong wind blowing from the south

C. The Lonely Life Of The Hawker

D.
1. hardy
2. isolated
3. tough
4. solitary

E. colour television, car, hamburger, ice cream, goldfish

THE DAYS OF THE HAWKERS EARNING A LIVING – ACTIVITY

1. pitchman
2. employer
3. wages
4. trade
5. dole
6. salary
7. resign
8. resume
9. vitae
10. intern
11. steward
12. promotion
13. apprentice
14. tinker
15. Maternity
16. peddler
17. employee
18. firm
19. redundant
20. commuter

PUZZLE 1. They know how to serve.

PUZZLE 2. He worked at the mint.

9. ELIZA DONNITHORNE COMPREHENSION

A.
1. Saint Stephen's Church, Newtown (Sydney)
2. Eliza's bridegroom did not arrive
3.
    a. the bridegroom had changed his mind about marrying Eliza
    b. he had been murdered
4. it was left to rot
5. she hoped her lover would return one day
6. Charles Dickens

B. No In the text it says it was a beautiful Spring day. June is a month of Winter.

C. Eliza Donnithorne, Charles Dickens, Major Thomas Mitchell, St Stephen's Curch, Newtown, Dunbar, Miss Havisham, Spring, Great Expectations

D. despair, sadness, grief, anguish, misery

E. Mystery Disappearance

Teacher: Discuss why the other two headlines are not plausible.

ELIZA DONNITHORNE – ACTIVITY TIME LINE

The Riddle Of The Rivers

As settlement spread from Sydney it followed inland rivers. Explorers who tried to find the mouths of these rivers were frustrated, either by rough terrain or disappearing in the vast MacQuarie Marshes. Charles Sturt was the first to find that these rivers were part of the Murray Darling system emptying into the ocean at Lake Alexandrina, South Australia.

10. FREDERICI'S GHOST COMPREHENSION

A.
1. Mr Frederici
2. Faust
3. Mephistopheles
4. he had a heart attack and died
5. they said been on the stage taking bows with him
6. in the dress circle

B. Yes Faust's deal was to exchange his soul for unlimited knowledge. Later we are told that he began his descent into Hell with Mephistopheles. This was the agreed price for the gift of unlimited knowledge.

C.
1. scholar
2. merely
3. baritone
4. dress circle

D. 'Mr Frederici, after being laid upon the floor, merely opened his eyes, looked up and closed them again.'

E.
1. opening
2. appreciative
3. evil
4. unexpected.

FREDERICI'S GHOST – ACTIVITY NAME THAT TUNE
1. God Defend New Zealand
2. Let Freedom Ring
3. Wimoweh
4. The Rose Of Tralee
5. Comin' Thro' The Rye
6. Picking Up Pebbles
7. At The Chocolate Bon Bon Ball
8. Blow the Wind Southerly
9. The Star Spangled Banner
10. Advance Australia Fair
11. Now Is The Hour
12. It's A Long Way To Tipperary

11. THE TANTANOOLA TIGER – COMPREHENSION

A.
1. South Australia
2. Bengal Tiger
3. sheep
4. humans
5. an Assyrian wolf
6. swum ashore from a shipwreck
7. Tantanoola's hotel
8. a tiger
9. more than 150
10. a corral with piles of bones lying around
11. a swaggie (swagman
12. stealing sheep

B.
1. ferocious
2. parties
3. predator
4. devouring
5. pursuers
6. corral
7. swaggie
8. sizeable

C. 1 = 4 2 = 5 3 = 1 4 = 3 5 = 2

THE TANTANOOLA TIGER – ACTIVITY
1. panther
2. puma
3. purr
4. veterinarian
5. mewing
6. Persian
7. licks
8. feline

PUZZLE: purple
9. tabby
10. leopard

11. lion
12. meowing
13. lynx
14. cheetah
15. Manx
16. tongue

PUZZLE: alley cat

17. kitten
18. felidae
19. tom
20. mouser

PUZZLE: kits

12. AUSTRALIAN ECCENTRICS #1
THE FLYING PIEMAN – COMPREHENSION

A.
1. someone who is different from most other people
2. non – conformist
3. William Francis King
4. physical fitness
5. London, 1807
6. 1829
7. Hope & Anchor Tavern
8. pies
9. Pies! Hot pies! Kidney, pork, apple, mutton! Hot pies!
10. Parramatta Steamer
11. 30 kilometres
12. an unsuccessful love affair
13. going on very long walks
14. coaches, ferries
15. using a clock to measure the time taken to run a distance
16. by betting on himself
17. 50 kilometres
18. he wore a blue jacket, bright red trousers and an old top hat with coloured streamers attached to it
19. an asylum in Liverpool in 1873
20. as a man with a gentle sense of fun

B.
1. earnings
2. mutton
3. kidney
4. pork
5. approximately
6. departed
7. disembarked
8. familiar
9. extraordinary
10. destitute

THE FLYING PIEMAN ENRICHMENT – ACTIVITY

A. restless hardworking busy unusual emotional

B.
1. pig
2. sheep
3. cattle (adult)
4. deer
5. chickens, ducks, geese, turkeys etc.
6. cattle (young)

C. teacher

D. teacher

13. AUSTRALIAN ECCENTRICS #2
HENRY GRIEN – COMPREHENSION

A.
1. Switzerland
2. England, South Africa
3. The Greatest Liar On Earth
4. a diving bell
5. they drowned
6. World Wide Magazine
7. Louis de Rougemont
8. The Adventures Of Louis de Rougemont As Told By Himself
9. in Australia's North East
10. dolphins and turtles
11. they could fly
12. underground burrows
13. a workhouse in Kensington, a suburb of London
14. he died penniless

B.
1. convincing
2. gullible
3. diving bell
4. reputable
5. dusk

HENRY GRIEN
HOAXES, FRAUDS & CHARLATANS

1. spaghetti
2. cheat
3. grafter
4. Caraboo
5. Piltdown
6. War Of The Worlds
7. counterfeit
8. Fiji Mermaid
9. nails
10. iceberg
11. Clever Hans
12. decimal
13. forgery
14. Mary Toft
15. platypus
16. gullible
17. fraud
18. ring – in
19. sucker
20. smellavision

PUZZLE: The Cottingley Fairies

14. AUSTRALIAN ECCENTRICS #3
SAMMY COX – COMPREHENSION

A.
1. 1773
2. he died when he fell from his horse while fox hunting
3. his uncle, John Jarvis
4. sea captain
5. taking him on a whale hunting expedition in the waters around Northern Tasmania
6. his uncle was going to abandon him so that he would inherit Sammy's property
7. he hid in the bush
8. he must have had an accident
9. sailed away without him
10. some aboriginal people living in the area
11. they made him a member of their tribe
12. 1806
13. Cox
14. gardener and handyman
15. 1891
16. 1
17. years

B.
1. wealthy
2. deserted
3. expedition
4. dreadful
5. incredible

C.
1. and
2. Both these headlines use the name Sammy Cox, a name Sammy adopted long after his disappearance and some time after living with the Cox family.

SAMMY COX ENRICHMENT ECCENTRICS # 3

A. teacher

B.
1. South Australia
2. Western Australia
3. Queensland
4. Northern Territory

C. Whales are mammals. They breathe with lungs. Because of these they must resurface to gather a breath. Fish are able to extract oxygen from water using their gills.

D.

15. AUSTRALIAN ECCENTRICS # 4
FRANCIS DE GROOT – COMPREHENSION

A.
1. Ireland
2. 1910
3. buying and selling antiques
4. English Royalty
5. The New Guard
6. Jack Lang
7. the ceremonial ribbon
8. a representative of the English Crown, the Governor General
9. a sword
10. 'On behalf of the decent, loyal citizens of New South Wales I declare this bridge open! '
11. he was arrested and fined
12. Ireland

B.
1. modest
2. royalty
3. like – minded
4. obscurity
5. prominence
6. staunch

C. taking action before a rival to gain an advantage

AUSTRALIAN ECCENTRICS CROSSWORD

See crossword answers at the back of this book.

16. ELIZA FRASER'S EXTRAORDINARY ORDEAL – COMPREHENSION

A.
1. 300 kilometres
2. whale and dolphin watching tours
3. K'gari
4. Paradise
5. Stirling Castle
6. seventeen
7. 1836
8. the baby died
9. Moreton Bay (Brisbane)
10. Great Sandy Island
11. ghosts of an enemy tribe
12. beaten and speared to death by aborigines
13. John Graham
14. white ghosts
15. eaten by a shark
16. The Mediterranean Packet
17. Alexander John Greene, the ship's captain
18. A Mother's Offering To Her Children
19. Charlotte Barton
20. a carriage accident in Melbourne

B.
1. Paradise
2. founder
3. castaways
4. therefore

ELIZA FRASER'S EXTRAORDINARY ORDEAL ENRICHMENT

A. Daniel Defoe

B.
1. Anna Sewell
2. Margaret Mahy
3. Hans Christian Andersen
4. J R R Tolkien
5. Enid Blyton
6. Jeff Kinney
7. Randolph Stow
8. Beatrix Potter
9. Roald Dahl
10. Jeff Brown

C. Hunter gatherers travel from place to place in search of food. Their food comes from wild plants and animals. Hunter gatherer societies were replaced by agricultural societies about 12 000 years ago.

D. teacher

17. P G TAYLOR – CROSSWORD

18. WHAT'S IN A NAME? – COMPREHENSION

A.
1. Norway
2. local aboriginal language
3. many of a certain thing
4. it reminded him of South Wales
5. battlegrounds
6. nearby shipwrecks
7. Bateau Bay
8. Illabo
9. Tom Huxley (a local resident)
10. null = no arbor = tree
11. Holbrook
12. Scotland

B.
1. consequences
2. numerous
3. mispronunciation
4. resident
5. daringly

C.

a. Woy Woy (___15___)
b. Wagga Wagga (___13___)
c. Walla Walla (___14___)
d. Cardiff (___5___)
e. Newcastle (___10___)
f. Swansea (___12___)
g. Perth (___11___)
h. Camperdown (___4___)
i. Cootamundra (___6___)
j. Balaklava (___2___)
k. Gosford (___7___)
l. Illabo (___9___)
m. Ballarat (___3___)
n. Albury (___1___)
o. Holbrook (___8___)

WHAT'S IN A NAME CAPITAL CITIES ENRICHMENT

C	O	T	S	B	E	A	B	E	I	J	I
K	N	C	A	N	R	R	B	U	E	G	N
H	E	N	J	A	K	A	Y	K	N	O	N
O	W	O	M	O	S	R	O	O	A	S	O
L	D	D	W	O	C	T	A	T	I	R	T
M	E	N	C	A	I	R	O	S	S	E	G
J	L	O	A	R	O	M	E	I	R	A	N
E	H	L	I	L	I	P	A	R	E	R	I
R	I	B	R	A	S	S	U	V	A	A	L
U	M	S	O	G	A	R	L	I	N	H	L
S	E	A	N	T	I	E	B	C	D	N	E
A	L	W	A	S	H	I	N	G	T	O	W

NOW MATCH EACH CAPITAL CITY WITH ITS COUNTRY.

1. London
2. Canberra
3. Brasilia
4. Beijing
5. Washington
6. Cairo
7. Wellington
8. Santiago
9. New Delhi
10. Buenos Aires
11. Berlin
12. Harare
13. Paris
14. Rome
15. Jakarta
16. Tokyo
17. Moscow
18. Rome
19. Jerusalem
20. Stockholm

19. GALMAHRA (JACKEY-JACKEY) & KENNEDY CROSSWORD

20. 'MUM SHIRL' SMITH COMPREHENSION

A.

1. Colleen Shirley Perry
2. fourteen
3. Budjarn
4. You have to first love yourself and spread it around.
5. Sydney
6. went to gaol
7. a Mum, mother
   a. Aboriginal Medical Service

B. teacher

C.

1. frequently
2. isolated
3. destructive
4. influenced

D. asp pass mass son cap pain main map nap pan passion snap amp camp icon coin scamp coop scoop snip spin spoon poison nip ass are a few

21. GRACE BUSSELL & SAM ISAACS – COMPREHENSION

A.

1. shipwreck
2. after
3. deed
4. strong
5. horse
6. waves
7. hours
8. honour

B.

1. Grace Darling
2. Western Australia
3. Busselton
4. Christmas pudding
5. stockman
6. Georgette
7. stirrups, reins, saddle leathers
8. teacher

C.

1. pioneers
2. heroic
3. exhausting
4. capsized
5. bronze
6. rescuing

D.

1. bravery
2. gallantry
3. heroism
4. valour

RESCUED ! teacher

22. AUSTRALIAN SONGBIRDS

A.

1. Helen Porter Mitchell
2. in honour of her home city, Melbourne
3. Europe
4. Peach Melba, Melba Toast
5. to announce one's departure or retirement but make many returns
6. they could be the equal of any in the world
7. Townsville
8. Our Glad
9. June Gough
10. Broken Hill
11. La Stupenda
12. the Wonderful One

B.
1. On The Road To Gundagai
2. Our Don Bradman
3. Advance Australia Fair
4. Waltzing Matilda
5. The Drover's Dream
6. I've Been Everywhere

C. STATEMENT: June Gough was born in Broken Hill.
QUESTION: Was June Bronhill born in Broken Hill?

D. population, farewell, pioneer, example, serving, gratitude, enriches

23. AUSTRALIAN QUEENS OF THE COURT – COMPREHENSION

A.
1. Smith
2. Goolagong
3. Albury, 1942
4. eleven
5. British Open
6. Australian, French, British, United States
7. Barellan
8. hitting a ball against a wooden fence
9. 19
10. Kelly
11. Dorothy Chalmers
12. 1914

B.
1. love
2. server
3. receiver
4. umpire
5. lob
6. doubles
7. Davis Cup
8. strings

C. teacher

D. teacher

24. AUSTRALIAN INVENTORS – WORKSHEET

A. Hugh Victor McKay = Sunshine Harvester Lance Hill = Hill's Hoist   Mervyn Victor Richardson = Victa lawnmower   Lewis Brandt = utility car   John Ridley = stripper - harvester Sunshine Bakeries = sliced bread   Maria Ann Smith – Granny Smith Apples   F G McEnroe = Chiko roll   L E de Mole = army tank Robert Bowyer Smith = stump jump plough

B.
a. Lyster
b. Brennan
c. Pavlova
d. Florey

C. and

D. teacher

25. SAME MESSAGE DIFFERENT METHODS – COMPREHENSION

A.
1. Reverend Richard Johnson
2. kind, gentle
3. weakness
4. by attending services
5. Governor Hunter
6. it kept the convicts in order
7. it was burnt down by a convict
8. he ordered that convicts attend church twice on Sundays
9. a sandstone storehouse
10. 1800
11. Reverend Samuel Marsden
12. he was more difficult to deal with than Johnson
13. Marsden dragged him ashore and flogged him
14. The Flogging Parson
15. they were impressed by him / respected him

B. Bahai Buddhism Christianity Confucianism Hare Krishna Hinduism Islam Judaism Shinto Sikhism Taoism are a few.

C.
1. An atheist does not believe in God or gods.
2. An agnostic neither believes nor disbelieves in God. They simply do not know

D.
1. seldom
2. thereafter
3. magistrate
4. Maori

26. FANNY DURACK – COMPREHENSION

A.
1. Sydney, 1891
2. unladylike
3. they had a 'Lady's Hour'
4. an hour during which ladies are allowed to participate in something normally allowed only to men
5. she taught herself
6. Coogee Baths
7. trudgen
8. any stroke
9. Australian crawl, front crawl
10. Annette Kellerman
11. Clevelend Street Baths, Sydney
12. 33 yards (30 metres)
13. Mina Wylie
14. Alec Wickham, Cecil Healey
15. six seconds
16. Stockholm
17. one
18. Mrs Hugh D McIntosh
19. win an Olympic gold medal

20. World War I
21. an attack of appendicitis
22. Wagga

B.
1. best thing since sliced bread, on fire
2. Rugby League was the winner
3. pin drop
4. 110%
5. like a man possessed

27. LASSETER'S GOLD REEF – FACT OR FICTION
1. BALL
2. EARLY
3. JOBS
4. OFTEN
5. CLAIMED
6. CENTRAL
7. LEADING
8. VANISHED
9. TRACE
10. BODY
11. DESERT
12. BURIED
13. PETERMANN
14. AVAIL
15. BELIEVE
16. REALLY
17. EXIST

27. CRICKET AUSTRALIA'S NATIONAL GAME COMPREHENSION
1. cricket
2. ten
3. Play up! play up! and play the game!
4. the torch of life
5. Henry Newbolt
6. 1892
7. a soldier
8. it is played in all Australia's states and territories
9. 1826
10. people gambled on the result
11. Sydney Gazette
12. 1851
13. Victoria and Tasmania
14. Launceston
15. Tasmania
16. a bugle
17. £ 500 ($1 000)
18. New South Wales
19. 18
20. England
21. England
22. 1868
23. Won = 14 Lost = 14 Drawn = 19
24. 1877

CRICKET AUSTRALIA'S NATIONAL GAME ENRICHMENT
A. Three Letters:
   a. gum
   b. ash
   c. oak
   d. fir
   e. yew
   f. elm

Four Letters:
   a. teak
   b. palm
   c. plum
   d. pear
   e. date
   f. pine

B. cedar
C. maple
D.
   a. caught
   b. bowled
   c. stumped
   d. run out
   e. leg before wicket
E. the cricket cap worn by Australian test match players
F. to administer the laws of the game
G. the wooden bars that rest on top of the stumps in cricket
H. You hit the ball to the fence (4 runs) or over the fence on the full (6 runs).
I. How's that? (Howzat?)